WINNING IS CONTAGIOUS

101 Practical Lessons To Help You Win
At The Game Of Life

by
Jeannie Skiffington
Motivational Speaker, Trainer, and Author
Member of the National Speakers Association

First Edition

Winning Track Press
P. O. Box 204, East Amherst, New York 14051
www.winningtrackpress.com

Winning Is Contagious
101 Practical Lessons To Help You
Win At The Game Of Life
by Jeannie Skiffington

Published by:
Winning Track Press
P. O. Box 204
East Amherst, New York 14051
U. S. A.

Website: www.winningtrackpress.com
E-Mail Ordering: winningtrackpress@att.net

Cover Design by Mari Anderson, Lights On Graphics
www.lightsongraphics.com

Copy Editing by Steve Skiffington, Ph.D.
Copy Editing by Maryann Lauricella
Copy Editing by Cathy Engstrom

Illustrations by Allison Mora

ISBN, print ed.   0-9722033-0-3

Library of Congress Cataloging-in-Publication Data
Skiffington, Jeannie
Winning is contagious: 101 practical lessons to help you win at the game of life/Jeannie Skiffington.
First edition.
ISBN   9-0722033-0-3

2002108461 CIP

Book Order Form

Honor Someone You Care About
Unique Gifts For Special People And Special Occasions

<u>SHIP TO:</u> (Please Include Phone # Or E-mail Address)

_____

_____

_____

_____

Call or Fax This Form To: 716-688-5507
E-Mail Order: winningtrackpress@att.net
Mail To: Winning Track Press
              P. O. Box 204
              East Amherst, New York 14051

_____**# of Books at $19.95 each** $_____
            (Call For Volume Discounts)
Shipping: $4.00 for the first book and
            $1.00 for each additional $_____

                              Subtotal $_____
Make Check Payable To: Tax 8%
Winning Track Press   (NY only) $_____

Credit Card # :   **Total** $_____

— — — — — — — — — — — — — — — — — — — —

Exp: ___ ___ *Name on Card:*_____

BOOKING JEANNIE IS EASY!

*"Let Jeannie's MAGIC rub off on your
company or association."*

Keynotes, Retreats, Workshops,
Annual Meetings, Conferences,
In-House Training, Full-Day Seminars

Jeannie Skiffington
Motivational Speaker/Trainer/Author
Rave Reviews Nationwide Since 1990
Member of the National Speakers Association

Website: www.winningiscontagious.com
"Bringing out the winner in everyone"
Call: 716-688-5507

She *Walks The Talk* With These Topics:
*Sales, Customer Service, Communication,
Leadership, Professionalism, Time Management,
Phone Skills, Change, Stress Management,
Team Building, Supervision, and
Business Building For Direct Sales*

**Look For My Next Book Coming Out
In The Spring of 2003:**

Winning Is Contagious At Work
101 Performance Standards To Achieve Professional Success

CONTENTS

Dedicated with love

To my Mom and Dad
for giving me roots and wings

To my husband, Steve,
for always cheering
on my efforts

To my children,
Christine and Joel,
who are the wind
beneath my wings

To my grandchildren,
Jacob and Alec
(and those to come)
who are absolutely the
stadium lights in my life

"The greatest gifts you can give your children are the roots of responsibility and the wings of independence."
Denis Waitley

FOREWARD

Jeannie and I have been married since 1991. Of course I am biased, but everyone who meets her realizes immediately that she is a very special lady! She loves people and life, is intelligent, assertive, charming, witty, kind, and enthusiastic, has integrity, is a go-getter, and has a "way with words." She believes in people and always goes the extra mile for others. She's always trying to improve herself, doing her best to turn a negative into a positive, and looking for the silver lining in the dark clouds. She practices what she preaches and has poured her heart and soul into this book. Jeannie communicates her contagious winner thinking in each of her 101 life lessons for winning at the game of life. She describes how others have deeply touched and helped her succeed. Her goal in writing this book is to help others succeed. Her writing is humorous and inspirational. She describes how she and many of the people she has known during her life have overcome adversity. Jeannie can relate to people facing challenges and obstacles because she has faced many in her own life. In this book, Jeannie advocates taking responsibility, setting goals, associating with high quality people, giving support to others, using winner thinking, using one's personal power, taking advantage of opportunity, taking risks, and turning negatives into positives along with a multitude of other strategies for achieving success. Jeannie's writing is like a breath of fresh air. Her home-grown wisdom and winning philosophy of life will help bring out the winner in you! You'll discover that, in Jeannie's words, "Winning is contagious!"

Steve Skiffington, Ph.D.
Clinical Psychologist

ABOUT THE AUTHOR

Jeannie grew up in an old mill town in New England after World War II, where everyone worked very hard and struggled daily just to get by. Poverty and the ravages of the war spun a web of trauma throughout her childhood. College was never an option. Struggling to make ends meet was all she knew. Goal setting included getting three "squares" a day, a roof over your head, marriage, and kids. There were no further instructions. Repeating history was a glaring reality.

As a wife and young mother of two children in the '60s, Jeannie traded in her apron and cookie sheets when her children entered school. Armed only with a high school diploma and a lot of determination to change the course of history for herself and her family, she achieved award winning success for 20 years in the direct selling industry before becoming a speaker, trainer, and author.

Jeannie has turned obstacles into a springboard to success and an opportunity to rise above life's challenges. She learned to open her own doors, set higher goals, and develop her drive and potential in a quest for professional excellence. Her enthusiasm and high energy are infectious, invigorating, and inspirational. She has beaten the odds, stacked them in her favor, and developed a passion for helping others do the same. Having been exposed to excellent training, great speakers, and positive mentors throughout her career, Jeannie realizes the value of awareness, knowledge, understanding, high impact, and repetition as critical ingredients to success.

As a self-made woman who has consistently succeeded despite poverty, childhood trauma, lack of educational opportunities, divorce, and cancer, Jeannie teaches the habits, qualities, and winner thinking needed for achieving outstanding success and professional excellence. She'll help you picture yourself a winner! Her energy and enthusiasm rub off on her audiences. With an Erma Bombeck style, she tells it like it is using real-life experiences with a down-to-earth approach. She succeeds in bringing out the best in people and inspiring them to make the real changes needed for their own success. She's entertainment with a power-packed message! She is a take-charge lady who makes things happen!

Jeannie has traveled this country extensively since 1993 presenting a wide variety of topics including sales, customer service, time management, leadership, empowerment, communication, team building, and motivation. Her topic diversity, personal and professional successes, humor, down-to-earth approach, savvy, and real life application make for direct-hit motivation every time!

"Winning is not what the world gives you,
it's what you give yourself."
Jeannie Skiffington

WITH GRATEFUL THANKS
TO THE WINNERS WHO PASSED IT ON

This book is my way of passing on all the wonderful information that I have learned, discovered, and delivered to audiences everywhere. My hope is that it is used as a tool to help you and the people you care about stack the odds in your favor to build *winning* outcomes. It's about giving back, in some small way, some of which has been given to me so caringly.

As I look back over my own career and personal life, I realize that my personal successes are really a combination of my ability and talent matched up with the lessons I learned from so many people. I've always said that I'm not so smart as I am a quick study. You show me and I can repeat it. The difference is that I applied what I learned with immediacy and passion. I am painfully aware that my ability and talent could just as easily have remained dormant were it not for some very specific defining moments captured during my life experience. These changed the course of events for the positive for me.

One challenge we all face is a lack of understanding over dilemmas and solutions for those dilemmas. We can all have numerous issues at the back of our minds that just nag at us. Essentially, we don't know what we don't know. Many of life's lessons come from the school of hard knocks. Surely I've earned my Ph.D. by now. I'm hoping that within these 101 lessons there might be that piece of wisdom, lesson, story, or personal experience that unlocks the mystery of understanding for some of the nagging issues you have or have had. My wish is that this book helps turn on a light of wisdom so that your dreams and goals might become reality.

Or, you just plain feel good about what you've learned and how you've developed your winning approach.

This book is also a tribute to the many winners who have taught me something I didn't know. It's a compilation of the wonderful lessons I've learned so far. It's my way of thanking them for sharing their insights and wisdom to help others win too. It's amazing how much of who I am has been a result of my associations with people personally and professionally. My inspiration has come from so many. I hold these people in the highest regard.

Sister St. Matthew taught me to compete with myself and to excel (and this one could have been a real sleeper). Without this one in place, I'm not sure the rest would have had the same impact. (1962-1963)

Tupperware Home Parties taught me how to set goals for building my own business. It stood for the highest standards of excellence in customer service, product quality, and integrity. During its first 30 years, it doubled six times every five years. What a privilege it was for me to be a part of that "Cinderella Story". Tupperware Home Parties did more to liberate women after World War II than anything else affecting my young adult life. The home party plan business expanded our options as entrepreneurs. The skills I learned by that association helped me open my own doors for the first time at age 25 and I haven't turned back since. I will be forever grateful for having been a part of its winning success story. (1972-1992)

Lauraine Blier was one sharp lady I met in 1972. She was a winning role model for sales, integrity, and class. She gave me the inspiration and motivation to say, "I can do what she does." She taught me that selling can be lucrative and successful and that you can be number one in sales without being pushy and obnoxious. She was the first person in business to see more in me than I saw in myself. She taught me to believe in myself. (1972)

Tom Damigella, Sr. was the first self-made millionaire businessman I had ever met. He was a pioneer with Earl Tupper in 1947 when Tupperware was born. He had been at the forefront of selling Tupperware in Boston, Massachusetts before it became home parties. He was a part of Tupperware's success story practically from day one. He single handedly dismantled my mistaken image of what the rich were like. He wowed me for years with his vision and wisdom. He was the first person I ever knew to share philosophy and deliver it in such an inspiring way. He taught me how to *think and think big*. Tom helped me understand business. He helped me understand (though difficult) to not give importance to something that's not important. Where would I be without learning those lessons from him? (1972)

Tommy Damigella, Tom's son, has carried the torch for the Damigella legacy with Tupperware for the last thirty years. He was the first person to treat me like a gold medal athlete in my sales career. For the first time in my life, I learned I could be anything I wanted to be, be the best, be number one, and build a very successful business. Under his guiding hand, caring support, and influence, I turned the corner of my life at age 29 and took charge of the person I was capable of becoming. He helped me change the course of history for my family. He and his dad taught me class with integrity. How grateful I am for knowing them both. They are living examples that winning is contagious and I'm living proof. (1976)

Helene Phifer was my inspiration to become a speaker. She was an international corporate trainer whom I had the privilege to learn from. She delivered information so beautifully and caringly. I hung on her every word and so admired her insight, social skills, and understanding for healthy and positive living. She had an incredible ability to get through to her audiences. She was my winning role model as a speaker. (1985)

Joe Hara was a self-made millionaire and outstanding businessman from Chicago who also was a pioneer in the early days with Tupperware. He rose to become the International President of Tupperware Home Parties in the '80s. Joe was an awe inspiring role model who taught me that no matter how high up the ladder of success you climb, people remain your number one priority. We felt it everyday from Joe. He personally signed (with notes) Christmas cards to every executive in the company year after year. To this day, when I send Christmas cards, I think of Joe. He didn't send cards because he had to. It wasn't a chore to him. He sent cards because he cared and wanted to show it. He knew every one of us by name. How fortunate I was to have rubbed elbows with Joe (never Mr. Hara). (1980)

Gaylin Olson, the current Group President for Latin America and Asia Pacific for Tupperware, helped me understand that when you're *ahead of your time*, popular opinion might not be on your side. I had never thought of that and it was a great consolation to me. I struggled with how to deal with my natural creativity. I was able to be true to myself, worry less about popular opinion, and let history "right it."

Since 1990, the National Speakers Association (NSA) has inspired me to build my speaking business. NSA's winning role models and standards of excellence for speakers are evident in the way it nurtures, builds, and helps new speakers develop their passion and build their business with integrity and class. Without NSA, I would be reinventing the wheel.

Elinor Basso, a Vice President for Dun & Bradstreet Business Education Services, always took such care to assure that the best quality and highest integrity were the hallmarks of her speakers. I learned a great deal from our six winning years together. I have the fondest memories. (1993)

Dr. Francis and Rosanne D'Ambrosio, my long-time friends, have inspired and taught me how to win in the face of personal tragedy in dealing with their severely handicapped child by caring for their child at home, greatly enhancing the quality of his life, and far exceeding his life expectancy. They have worked miracles and have been a real inspiration for the last 20 years.

Sue and Bob McLanahan have maintained winning standards for their special child for the last 15 years by not giving up, not giving in, and realizing marvelous victories for their daughter, while maintaining quality in their lifestyle as a family.

I'm currently choosing my sensational senior role models. They're the people I want to be like when I get older. Dr. Nelson Ribble, Emma Melancon, Helene and Warren Phifer, Tom Damigella, and Jo Biondolillo are at the top of my list. They represent almost 500 years of winning, great attitudes, energy for living, grace, and dignity for growing older!

There are so many more people from whom I've learned wonderful lessons. I thank them and those I will continue to learn from because I'm certainly not done yet. I hope you're not done either. Together we can unlock some of life's *simple* mysteries (simple after you figure it out of course). Information is everywhere and I'm in constant pursuit of those puzzle pieces that can help us be happier and more successful for ourselves, our families, and the legacy we leave behind to build a better world. WINNING IS CONTAGIOUS! Let's help each other catch it and pass it on!

LESSON #1

ONCE UPON A TIME

Once upon a time a little girl was born in an old mill town in New England after World War II. She was born breech so the struggle began early. But there was an interesting coincidence. She was also the first born on January 1, 1947. Parents were young and had traditional values. Dad worked and Mom stayed home. Dad returned from World War II and they married 45 days later. This little girl was born 14 months after that. We had won the war and everyone returned home to work. Life went on.

However, the ravages of war were not far away. Dad had spent a challenging childhood before going to war at the tender age of 21. He saw the beaches of Normandy, was wounded twice and sent back, and marched across Europe carrying an 80-pound mortar to help defeat the German Army. My Mom was the sixth of seven girls and was the first in her family to complete high school. She was still a teenager when she went to work in the factories sewing parachutes for the war effort. They were kids with awfully big shoes to fill. Success meant winning World War II.

Life continued on and some of Dad's wartime habits, including smoking and drinking, found their way more and more into our daily lives. Money became scarce, poverty was our lot, and stress and struggle were everyday occurrences.

Everyone in that old mill town was pretty much first generation American. Their parents had come seeking work and a new life in the early 1900s during the Industrial Revolution. People were starting over and everyone worked in the mills.

This was a blue collar environment of hard workers who were making *ends meet*. My generation was pretty much born there, brought up there, and stayed there. We got jobs by referral from someone who knew someone looking for someone. No one ventured too far from the comfort of that mill town. That little girl who grew up (under duress) could just as easily have followed in the most obvious of footsteps. Finish school, get a job, get married, have kids, and save for a 25th anniversary trip to Orlando, Florida. It was what everyone did. And, after all, was that so bad? People who have money have problems anyway. This life was simple, easy, and a no-brainer. All success meant was that we struggled a little less than our parents. But somehow, we were vested in struggling. Could the chain be broken? We had no formal education after high school. Opportunities were in the mills. And, after all, was that so bad? People found happiness despite the struggle. And so, a life was born, built, and ended in that old mill town.

STOP THE WORLD, I WANT TO GET OFF! REWIND! WHAT DO I DO WITH THOSE THOUGHTS OF YEARNING FOR MORE? WHAT DO I DO WITH THE QUESTIONS OF HOW PEOPLE WHO HAVE MORE GET IT? IS THERE SOMETHING BETTER? IS IT POSSIBLE TO LEARN THAT? CAN I POSSIBLY CHANGE THE COURSE OF HISTORY FOR MY FAMILY? PROBABLY NOT. AFTER ALL, I DON'T KNOW WHAT I DON'T KNOW. AND WORSE, I DON'T KNOW WHERE TO FIND IT OR GET IT. OH, ONE MORE PROBLEM IS THAT I DON'T KNOW ANYONE WHO CAN TEACH ME, TELL ME, OR SHOW ME. I JUST DON'T KNOW ANYONE DIFFERENT THAN ME! NO ONE EVER TOLD ME I COULD BE ANYTHING I WANTED TO BE. THIS IS ALL I KNOW! WHERE DO I BEGIN? WHAT DO I DO?

Many of us can have these feelings and often the best consolation we get from the people who know us and love us is, "Well, it's not so bad. Why not just do what everybody else does? Everybody can't all be wrong. What we have is good enough. You'll get over it."

STOP THE WORLD IF YOU WANT TO GET OFF! YOU CAN REWIND! YOU DO HAVE A CHOICE! LIFE CAN BE BETTER. PURSUING ONE'S DREAMS IS SIMPLY A QUESTION OF LEARNING WHAT WE NEED FROM THE PEOPLE WHO HAVE DONE IT SUCCESSFULLY BEFORE US.

In this book are the 101 life lessons that this little girl learned to change the course of history, be true to herself, and develop a respect for her roots. Each of us has the responsibility to use and develop our potential to make this world a better place and to leave our mark on history, our families, our workplaces, and our friendships.

You too can STOP AND REWIND at any point in your life and become the person you truly want and deserve to be. Simply be willing to search for the information you need and rub elbows with those people who can help you *advance the cause*.

LESSON #2

DIFFICULTY CAN BE THE
SPRINGBOARD TO SUCCESS

I've come to look at struggle, challenge, and obstacles differently over the years. My previous thinking included something about "the rich get richer" or "it takes money to make money." Heard that more times than I care to remember. The implied message in those phrases is probably more damaging than most of us have ever considered. The implied message is that you must possess "richness" first in order to acquire more. So now we create the vicious cycle. You don't have and you'll never have. That's the way it is no matter what you do. It's easy to believe that. Conveniently, it lets us off the hook, doesn't it? I suppose there's not a lot to explain while we struggle with our lot in life. After all, we can at least get credit for doing a good job struggling can't we?

I remember as a child laying in bed when things got pretty rough and wondering, "why was I born?" Life certainly seemed a dead end. One thing that those times taught me for sure was that I didn't want them, and the agony helped form my convictions at a very early age about what I wanted and didn't want.

I remember my friend Vivian and how I used to fantasize about having her life. It was so normal in my eyes. I often spent Sunday afternoons with her, having dinner with her family. It was such a wonderful respite from reality. But all the while I was balancing mentally what was and what could be. My inner strength was slowly forming and growing. Yes, what I'm saying is that struggle and challenge can help build who you are and always with an eye toward what you want once you find the opportunity to springboard to a better place.

Great success stories most often begin with tragedy but end in a positive result. So, no matter what your struggle, challenge, or obstacle is you can begin to view it as a *springboard* to success, as you gain the insight and information you need to make your *leap to a better place*. Think of all the wonderful stories of people who have lost 100 pounds. That success could not have been achieved without first the challenge of being overweight. Who better can understand the struggle of overweight people than that person who has successfully struggled through it? My Dad's alcoholism was a tragedy but his success over tragedy made him "an instrument of peace." There's no one better to understand the downfalls of addiction than the person who has lived it and overcome it.

You see, this world cannot be a better place without first having real people struggle through real challenges to become unlikely heroes. They set the standards and reach out to help others find their way. Every one of us will face challenge. Our goal is to springboard to a better place and help form the standards from which others may inch their way to greater success.

LESSON #3

ARE HEROES BORN OR MADE?

In a nutshell, heroes are made every day from circumstances that are not selected but rather *thrown at them*. And they overcome them to the amazement sometimes of themselves and the rest of us who can't imagine successfully navigating through them.

It was a lesson I learned many years ago during the '60s while the war in Vietnam was going on. I was so taken by the young men my age who were captured and held as POWs for years in solitary confinement. In my late teens and early 20s, my mind could not fathom such a desperate set of circumstances. What was very interesting though was that upon their return from captivity, these POWs were greeted as heroes while at the same time insisting they were not and didn't feel like heroes.

I remember being so puzzled by their *take* on their set of circumstances. Why wouldn't you recognize being a hero? After all, it's what you look like to us, your fellow countrymen. But, indeed, the pain involved in living as a prisoner and knowing the personal day-to-day struggle just to survive doesn't exactly equate to the glamour often associated with the word *hero, success,* or *winning*. These prisoners saw their own *failure* in being captured. Then it becomes a real *leap* in their minds to get to the *hero thinking*.

Perhaps we don't feel worthy of such accolades. Trauma gets in the way of equating success with getting through and surviving terrible circumstances. I've come to believe that real heroes happen every day from the unlikeliest of candidates. They are those people who rise above the *muck and the mire* of everyday existence and ultimately find success, freedom, and choice. Heroes are not only born from wars, disease, rescues, and the Olympics, they're born from making the best of any bad situation we encounter day-to-day. They're the people who create an outcome that is beyond what most people are willing to settle for.

Every person born has the potential for beating the odds, exhibiting personal heroics, and winning personal achievement. Regardless of circumstances, it begins with believing in possibility by spending our lifetime, potential, and talent building our own *unique success story*. Some parts will not be pretty, which is why it's called a success story. Ultimately we leave this world a better place by inspiring those we rub elbows with.

Sometimes we are privileged to learn this lesson from our own families. Sometimes we don't learn this lesson from our families but instead we learn it from successful winners around us or from books. No matter where we learn this lesson, we must be open to discovering our inner self and the treasure buried down deep in us all.

LESSON #4

STOP THE BLAME GAME

Personal success and achievement can be thwarted or lost due to our own human reaction to obstacles and challenges that prevent a *straight shot* to success. We live in a world that spends too much time blaming and not enough time problem solving regarding our challenges and obstacles. We tend to perceive challenges and obstacles as reasons to retreat or give up or as indicating that it is not meant to be.

While there are certainly times when you hit a wall, if you logically approach obstacles as *factors to work around*, then you can inch your way closer to success and keep hope alive. Obstacles are what you see when you take your eyes off the goal. Keep your eyes on the goal, be persistent, don't panic, problem solve, and success remains in your grasp. The major difference between failure and success becomes how we view our circumstances and trust in our own potential to overcome those circumstances. How we react in the pursuit of our goals and dreams has very little to do with whether we personally created the challenge or it is dumped on us by our environment.

Personally and historically, we can look around and see those people who inspire us despite difficult circumstances. Stories become success stories when we see people overcome obstacles. So, in the end, the difference between winning and losing is how we view the possibilities in our circumstances rather than getting hung up on *who did it*, only to become controlled by the anger, agony, and frustration that result. What angers you controls you. We must instead recognize the reality of what happened, accept that we can't change the past, and immediately kick into problem solving mode by asking ourselves, for example, "What if I do this?" or "How else can I do that?"

Dr. Viktor Frankl, a psychiatrist and author who wrote *The Meaning of Life*, captured three very valuable points in his book on how to deal with difficulty. What made his writing so profound was that he was a prisoner who survived a German concentration camp during World War II. The three lessons he shares to deal with difficulty are:

1) Find a purpose in the challenge.

Become stronger, test your limits, learn something, or help others. For example, recovered alcoholics help and understand first hand the recovery of other alcoholics. People who successfully deal with weight loss help others be inspired as they share their tips and techniques. Likewise, Dr. Frankl captured for the world his survival skills.

2) Have a clear-cut vision of life after the difficulty.

Focus on getting through it. Distract yourself, change your own mind, and find the humor. Denis Waitley told the story of a Vietnam POW who, having been released after many years of solitary confinement, made a first request to play a game of golf. To the amazement of everyone, the man scored extremely well given the circumstances of his physical and mental state. When he was asked how he did it, his response was simply, "I played every day in my mind." This was obviously a critical survival skill he successfully implemented. Rather than becoming beaten by his circumstances, he created a world in which he could survive, a world in which he played golf.

3) Learn from your experience.

Ask yourself, "What did I learn from this?" Once you answer that question and develop some appreciation for the learning experience and the knowledge gained then MOVE ON! It will allow you to more successfully incorporate and accept it into your life experience and personal success story.

Bad things happen to everyone, even nice people who don't deserve it. That's just the way it is! I remember when growing up hearing people say they'd pray to God for things like perfect children, trouble-free lives, better jobs, or no sickness. I always wondered to myself if not you, then, whom will God give it to? Does your God have a list of his *favorites* or *privileged few* or the *rich*? Are you really asking God to give tragic events to someone else? Why exactly should God spare you from difficulty? Frankly, he didn't even spare his own Son! But, oh, the lessons we have all learned for over 2000 years from that influence.

The third point also means that we should not get caught up telling rotten stories over and over and over. We should not prolong our own pain, agony, and inability to get past it. We should successfully *compartmentalize* the event. We must learn to get past it and accept that it happened and can't be changed. We must learn that the future is ours to recapture and then move on. Our emotional side wants to cling to the pain and sadness, while our logical side struggles to emerge.

We could all tell story after story of trial, tribulation, and unfairness, personally or in the workplace. But the winner has developed the ability to successfully compartmentalize the challenge or obstacle to create a healthier perspective that allows him or her to move ahead rather than getting stuck in the blame game forever.

LESSON #5

ARE YOU AN ACCIDENTAL OR ON-PURPOSE SUCCESS?

Picture this. You're walking down the street one day and as you check the time on your wristwatch, you notice a $10 bill on the sidewalk. You pick it up, realizing that finding the owner is impossible, and say to yourself, "Wow! I found 10 bucks." You go the office and tell a few people of your lucky coincidence. You put the money in your pocket and for all intents and purposes your lucky coincidence is history! Six months later, someone at the office says to you, "Hey, what did you do with the 10 bucks you found that day a few months ago?" "Are you kidding?" you say. "How would I know?"

Now, picture this. You're walking down the street one day and as you check the time on your wristwatch, you notice a $10 bill on the sidewalk. You pick it up, realizing that finding the owner is impossible, and say to yourself, "Wow! I found 10 bucks." Once the "wow" wears off though, you say to yourself, "This 10 bucks is nothing I worked for. Finding it was just plain luck. I know what I'll do, I'll put it in the bank and leave it there for 20 years in a savings account and give it to my one-year-old at 21 years of age." Now, for 20 years you get a bank statement that says $10.85, $12.52, $14.89, etc. Then, at your 21-year-old's birthday, you present the "lucky break" from 20 years before with a note that says, "Everyone gets lucky breaks in life. It's all about what you do with them. You can make something of them or make nothing of them. But making something of them is certainly no accident."

You see, everyone has breaks in life. The challenge is in recognizing the possibility in the lucky break and seeing it for what it could become. Capitalizing on the special set of circumstances and taking it up a flagpole can make the difference between the person who is lucky and the person who is lucky and successful.

All too often we see "other people's breaks" as having value. We tend to minimize the value of our own breaks. Our breaks are nothing compared to *so and so's* breaks. Now, if I had their breaks, oh what I could do. Malarkey, malarkey, malarkey!

Once we learn the principle of making more of circumstances than meets the eye, we'll be well on our way to seeing the real "luck" of adding our own "potential" to the breaks we all get during our lives. We can all look back and see some breaks we missed taking advantage of. The good news is we should learn from that and be ever ready to take advantage of the next set of promising circumstances. Oh, and one more thing...breaks rarely come at a convenient time. That's what makes it even trickier but so exciting when we manage to pull that rabbit out of the proverbial hat! Luck and success are simply preparation meeting opportunity and shaking hands!

LESSON #6

OPPORTUNITY WEARS A DISGUISE

Imagine that "opportunity" is like a door-to-door salesman. You're living your life at home, moving at the speed of light, getting the important things done that need to get done, and all of a sudden the doorbell rings. You think to yourself, "Who in the heck is that now?" The sound of the doorbell certainly feels like an interruption while you're accomplishing what's really important to you that day at that time.

Opportunity is much the same as that door-to-door salesman. Opportunity creeps up everywhere but very often our inclination is to simply think, "No, not now. I'm busy." It's always interesting to me when I hear people say things like, "No, we've got a birthday that week, I don't think we can" or "No, got a doctor appointment that day, can't do it." Now, these are great excuses to "blow off" something you really want to avoid. However, more often than we realize, people don't even entertain the possibilities in their own minds or get creative about how they might have it all.

I must admit, I get a certain thrill out of figuring the *ins and outs* of pulling something off that seems inopportune. What's become interesting over the years is how many things I have managed to pull off just by putting my thinking cap on and actually considering possibilities. I guess I've come to learn that just maybe I CAN have it all! Giving up or giving in comes naturally. We've got to train ourselves otherwise.

This process is a great mental exercise in building personal creativity. We tend to be too complacent in accepting things as they are and even telling ourselves that it wasn't meant to be. You hear people say all the time, "Well, it just wasn't meant to be" when the truth is, much of it can be if we just get past this initial human reaction. Here are phrases that belie the best intentions. "I was going to call you." "I meant to do such and such." "I never got around to it." "We'll have to get together." These phrases often lack the action required to get past the hectic schedule and general life confusion to make them reality. We miss too much at the hands of "no time" or "didn't work out." Taking advantage of life's opportunities rarely comes gift-wrapped. Anything worthwhile will always feel like effort. Spontaneity develops our sense of adventure while preventing the same old, same old.

We need to be challenging ourselves by considering options that just might fly. Then we train ourselves to "believe in possibility" even when we already have plans. Be vigilant because opportunity knocks when we least expect it, have time for it, or think we need it. Keep a very watchful eye for the next time opportunity knocks!

LESSON #7

LIFE IS A-MAZE-ING

Wouldn't we all love a straight shot to success? Kind of like here's a piece of paper, now tell me what I should do. Wouldn't that be terrific? Well, truth is it probably wouldn't be terrific because we would remain dependent on people telling us what to do. Now, last time I checked, I'm not too thrilled with people telling me what to do.

We all would prefer avoiding unnecessary mistakes but the simple truth is *mistakes are part of discoveries.* I learned that from Dr. Roger Firestien, a creativity speaker in the Buffalo, New York area.

Life to me is like a *maze*. Think about it for a minute. Remember when you learned how to do mazes? You would look at the maze and try to find the *way out* with your *eye* before ever putting a pencil to paper. Once you begin with pencil to paper, convinced of course that you've already *eyeballed* it correctly, you realize that you haven't gotten too far before you hit obstacle number one. While you're busy scratching your head trying to figure out how you missed it, you probably find yourself backing up with your pencil and figuring a new way to escape. What's really happening is that you're figuring the maze out by *process of elimination.* You begin to learn where the obstacles are and you actually train your eye to look more clearly to reduce obstacles. Let's say you run into two or three more *walls* in the maze, here again you are narrowing your field of play to eliminate obstacles that help define the only way out.

Life is just like a *maze*. Talent alone is never enough. Education alone is never enough. Simply put, there is no substitute for wisdom or life experience which only come when we're *thrown into the field* to compare what knowledge and talent tell us to the reality of what we face. Too often, people chew themselves up and spit themselves out because they thought they were entitled to a straight shot out or up. Life just doesn't happen that way. We will all be challenged to figure it out at some point. Oh, and here's the other catch: no two people's *life mazes* are alike.

I remember my son telling me during his MBA graduate studies that one of the professors taught them this: "You can gain knowledge from other people's wisdom, but you cannot gain wisdom from other people's knowledge."

So get going because you have a *maze* to tackle. Obstacles may await for sure but LIFE IS A-MAZE-ING.

LESSON #8

ARE YOU PROACTIVE, REACTIVE, OR INACTIVE?

"Oh, that always happens." Really, why? Do we even realize when we make statements like this one that we have actually made an unconscious decision to live with it? We've made the decision to accept what has gone down even though we might not be particularly thrilled with it. As a matter of fact, it even seems as though we're building a thicker skin to accommodate and accept what happens.

Learning to be proactive is a life skill but it's probably not our first inclination. The human side doesn't want to be bothered. We just wish or hope it would happen otherwise. The old "shucks" approach. It just wasn't in the cards.

First, I think it's important to understand the difference among the three possibilities. I suppose you could make a case for the validity of each depending upon the circumstances with which you are faced. Anyhow, here's my best explanation for the three possibilities.

> Proactive people *make* things happen.
> Reactive people *wait* for things to happen.
> Inactive people say, *"What happened?"*

Picture a large clock with no hands on it, that is, just a circle with numbers on it. Now, when something doesn't matter to you one way or the other, I suppose taking an inactive approach is much like this clock. You become oblivious to time. The clock is useless. The input of information doesn't change the outcome.

Now, picture the same large clock but this time with numbers and hands on it and sweat pouring off this clock. The stress is mounting. This can illustrate the reactive mode when we're just trying to catch up, squeeze in one more thing, or doing the "oops, uh-oh" banana-peel approach to life or work. We may be successful but at an unnecessary price.

Now, picture the same large clock but this time with numbers and hands on it and, instead of sweat, a big smile on the clock's face. This picture can depict that "winner" who has come to understand that unpredictable circumstances can become more predictable as we develop and build awareness of how they occurred and what the causes might be. The proactive person is keenly aware of the tiny changes that can easily be implemented before something becomes a *bigger nut to crack.*

I've always known that tiny mistakes can come back and haunt you and you're never aware that it came from a simple tiny oversight. Being vigilant as to the workings of our lives, workplaces, or our homes is the key to unlocking a proactive approach to preventive maintenance in our daily struggles.

I was recently in a McDonald's play area with my youngest grandson when a younger mother of two began chatting with me. She was mentioning how difficult it was parking and coming in to the McDonald's with a two-year-old and an infant in a baby carrier seat during wintertime. As she was preparing to leave, she announced to her two-year-old in a rather non-definitive ho-hum way that they were leaving. As she got the baby ready to go, she began searching in this rather large McDonald's play area for her two-year-old. As she called out her name, the two-year-old was nowhere to be found and apparently well hidden in the play area. The mother then said to those of us around who were within hearing distance, "Oh, she always does that." Then the Mom enlisted the aid of several older children to go find the little girl dressed in pink. Once again, this plan faltered too. Eventually, the mother retrieved the child after about 10 to 15 minutes and the child was screaming over her capture. The mother was struggling (against the odds) to get winter clothes on her daughter. It was apparent the mother was somewhat embarrassed at the scene. As we made eye contact, the mother said to me, "I should have spanked her, shouldn't I?" I thought to myself, "No, spanking is a reactive approach to a problem unsolved." As a matter of fact, the mother took a quite passive approach, given the play area scenario and the ability of a two-year-old to comply. So, the proactive approach in this scenario, given the previous history of "she always does that," is simply to outsmart the two-year-old by withholding the announcement of departure. Simply plan for the next time the child comes out of the play area closest to your departure time and start to put on their jacket. You can begin delivering the motivation for the next exciting part of their day and their role in it.

This was a clear cut example of giving the two-year-old so much leeway that the child began to lead the adult while the adult thought the child was misbehaving. The child was simply taking advantage of a big loophole the mother provided in her passive approach. It makes the two-year-old more clever than the parent.

Life is a choice. We either go along with the program passively, fix something after it happens for the 80th time, or we can decide to solve the situation by preventing it from occurring in the first place and bring closure to a set of circumstances.

Becoming proactive takes practice, persistence, and creativity. The more we successfully navigate through unpleasant circumstances, the more we develop the proactive high-achiever mentality that is key to getting past life's challenges and obstacles instead of getting taken down by them. Being proactive goes to the heart of personal achievement to prevent burnout, boredom, and the *woe is me* attitude. Luck can be made when you develop a proactive approach every single day that will create a better quality existence. Singularly, it can make the difference between wishing for something and getting something.

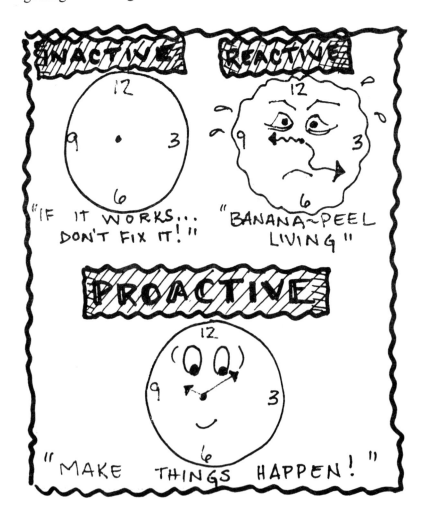

LESSON #9

ARE YOU A PESSIMIST OR AN OPTIMIST?

As human beings, I suppose it's pretty natural to be pessimistic. My guess is that we human beings have to work at being optimistic. Now, it's real easy being optimistic when the Publishers Clearing House Prize Patrol pulls up to your house on Super Bowl Sunday to announce you're the new Million Dollar Prize Winner. Short of that, however, we're left on our own day-to-day and without the million dollars.

Here's how I like to describe the pessimist. Pessimists are those who have become so negative that they start figuring out what the epitaph on their tombstone ought to say when they die. They tend to have a doomsday mentality. Their approach to life is "It's not going to work" or "It doesn't matter anyway." The pessimist is the person whose tombstone could easily read, "I knew this would happen." What I've discovered about pessimists is that they can be nice people who make you laugh over their doldrum stories. It's just that when you're done interacting with them, you tend to feel worse than before you interacted with them. It's the old *misery loves company (and approval)* approach. This group seeks out audiences who let them tell their miserable tales of woe over and over again. Their lives are comprised of one complicated sob story after the other. It's almost as if unconsciously they've resigned themselves to not being the picture of success so they have now embarked on the task of being the best picture of disaster. Some people will get recognition any way they possibly can. Of course, these are not the folks you want a steady day-to-day diet of. Otherwise your struggle becomes even more of a struggle. Hope is just sucked right out of you rubbing elbows with these characters.

Remember, just liking people is not reason enough to hang out with them. We need to give each other's existence VALUE and a lot more value than misery.

The optimist, on the other hand, chooses not to focus on disaster. The optimist will focus on creativity, improvement, and persistence, and believe in the ability to problem solve to get to a better place. If this optimist chose an epitaph for a tombstone, it could easily read, "The best is yet to come." I've said this so many times in my speaking career that I suppose I ought to adopt the saying as my epitaph. But, you see, this whole example isn't about tombstones or dying. It's really about how we look at the future, possibility, and our own potential to make things better. What we need to learn is to focus on the positive and possibilities, 24/7, to survive. I don't believe this comes naturally to human beings. We most definitely have to train ourselves and observe the heroes among us who have developed an optimistic approach. Much of this book is devoted to the thinking we need to develop and practice to maintain and protect our attitude. We must be ever mindful of that *check up from the neck up*. Be brave enough to cut yourself loose from the *toxic people* in your lives, and develop those relationships that give added value and meaning to your existence. Then practice, practice, practice.

LESSON #10

EXACTLY WHAT
ARE YOU SHOOTING FOR?

Struggle begets struggle and winning breeds winning. Simple enough. Now picture this. You look up at a marvelous tall bookcase that goes up 20 feet. On each of its shelves is a different more beautiful gift the higher up the shelves you go. This illustration reminds me so much of those times growing up when we asked ourselves, "Who on earth can afford a house like that?" "Where do they get the money?" "Where do these people come from?" All the while we are reinforcing our own thinking that it all feels so impossible to achieve.

Many of us growing up in that old mill town in the '50s were either poor or poorer. Take your pick. People worked in the mills making dresses, lingerie, or shoes. They were busy rebuilding a new life in America after World War II. I grew up hearing phrases like, "We don't have much but we eat good" or "Get yourself three squares a day, a roof over your head, and a husband that doesn't run around." Believe me when I tell you, those phrases made complete sense to me growing up. I saw them as pretty darned good wisdom.

As I reflect on where I come from and where I've been, it occurs to me that what I was taught in that old mill town in those first 20 years of my existence were pretty basic goals to shoot for. They were valid but indeed basic. I grew up surrounded by people who had no clue how to improve their day-to-day existence. As a matter of fact, I remember very clearly learning that "people with money have problems" which was an obvious reference to the view that our poverty problems were easier to deal with than *big money* problems.

I must admit that even at a tender young age that thought puzzled me. It just didn't seem to make any sense. It seemed to me that *a little more money* would be a happy medium to reduce the struggle. But what did I know? I was a kid.

I looked up to adults and depended on them to steer me in the right direction. Then again, my guess is they were sharing with us everything they knew, however much that was. And so, we lived and struggled to make *ends meet*. I can remember times in my 30s when I would give my mother a gift that she would never buy herself. After opening it, absolutely thrilled, she'd say something like, "Oh, Jeannie, that's beautiful. I think I'll put it away for when I go to the hospital." I'd have to say, "Ma, wear it. We'll get more if you go to the hospital." I always get a laugh from audiences when I tell this story because my guess is many of us have heard something like that from our parents or relatives. I remember Nana who lived in Middlebury, Vermont in the '70s. She had terrible arthritis in her legs and could no longer get out like she used to. She therefore watched lots of TV during the day. I remember her saying, "Oh, I would love a new color TV." Of course, she'd say it but would deny it to herself until the day she died. This was the hardworking, defer to everyone else, and get by making *ends meet* population. They were very good at struggling. They could squeeze a nickel like no one I know today. Hmm, sounds like a lesson that needs to be reborn. What do you think?

Anyhow, back to my bookshelf. After you decide what you're really shooting for, picture that bookshelf again. There may be a lot of goals that seem unattainable from where you stand now. It'd be like looking up at that 20-foot bookshelf that sure has some interesting beautiful gifts on those top shelves. Maybe what you learned in your early years reflects some of the basic goals outlined in this lesson.

Let's just say that the gifts on the lower shelves represent the basic needs in life like food, shelter, and relationships. Especially if you haven't had *further instructions*, it's very easy to settle in, get comfortable, and be reasonably satisfied with your basic happiness. Now, this example is not just about what makes you happy. It's about knowing how to reach the top shelf if you choose to. We can't ever stifle ourselves by not learning and appreciating how we can reach any goal. I can remember in high school when there was not even a question of going to college for most of us. The topic was never entertained, pursued, or even brought up. In my mind, there was no possibility or even need for it. Period.

So when I began in business for myself in 1972, I discovered something. I didn't know how to set goals without worrying what would happen if I didn't make them. I found myself trying to play it safe because security in the world I knew was not easy to let go. Frankly, it was frightening. We often limit ourselves and are not entirely sure why. We just think, that's not for me, when deep down we really want it but are afraid to embrace the possibility. So we decide to play it safe.

Life and achievement can be so exciting. Sometimes we have no idea how to achieve something. The speaking business that I started from scratch in 1990 certainly fell into this category. Luckily for me, I had already been exposed in my earlier business successes to reaching higher and higher and figuring it out as I go. I learned to be true to my goals and dreams and not get caught up in sidelining them. Writing this first book is a stretch for me. I suppose it's a natural spinoff to a speaking business. I know I have to become an *author* to achieve the next level. But, can I honestly tell you at this writing that I feel like an author or fit the picture of an author in my own mind? The answer is no, but I will stretch and figure it out as I go. The bottom line is that maybe you're shooting for goals that are too low or too basic to keep yourself interested in achievement. We set goals for two reasons: *to reach them and to stretch.*

We learn as we go by building our potential and gaining confidence in our ability to be courageous enough to step outside the world we know to create the world we want to grow into.

LESSON #11

FILLING IN THE BLANKS

As you look back on what you were taught in your first 20 years, perhaps you look back with fondness and pride. Or maybe you look back and feel like you missed out on lots of things. Perhaps you look back and appreciate what you did receive but still wonder *what if* you had had the benefits others had.

While the *bloom where you're planted* approach seems rather cut and dried, sometimes leaving us wishing we had been planted in a better situation, I have come to one very comforting conclusion. Looking back upon my own personal successes, it occurs to me that I was able to successfully grasp the *what was and what wasn't* in my early development. By taking stock of what I felt I needed or wanted, I was able to embark on the journey of *filling in the blanks* while still developing a healthy respect for the past.

Our goal from about age 20 on up should be to *fill in the blanks* as we go. We should constantly be testing and affirming whatever we learned early on to see if it still remains part of who we are and who we want/need to be given current circumstances. It's so easy to look around and wonder why we weren't *discovered* walking down the street and why we aren't pursued like some seem to be. What do others have that we don't have?

It's so easy to give up or not try for something because we see ourselves as missing certain key pieces or we don't have what others had to get there in the first place. Phrases like *the rich get richer* have a way of implying that if you're not born rich, then you're left to buying lottery tickets for the rest of your life. Oh well!

The truth is we must dedicate ourselves to use the example of the "rich get richer" to finding out who among the *rich* wasn't *rich* to begin with. We must empower ourselves with the knowledge of how the *rich* think, achieved, and built their success. We must be committed to studying the topic until we find the piece that is eluding us.

While we certainly need to play the hand we've been dealt, we must remember there's a deck to choose from, and from which winning combinations can come. We must be ready and on the lookout to add to the *hand we were dealt* and be in hot pursuit of the cards we haven't found yet that will create our own winning hand. As in that card game, we are constantly considering new strategies as cards get played. All the while we're looking for the card that advances our position to a win. In a way, we are competing with ourselves as well as with others. While we can all wish that things were a certain way, it is more important to get out there and *fill in the blanks* to help those wishes come true. Then, and only then, you create your own unique success story. While we can learn from others, we must figure it out for ourselves. And we will when we consistently work at adding to our knowledge and experience base by *filling in the blanks.*

LESSON #12

WHAT IS WINNING ANYWAY?

Winning, when you look around the world we live in, can come to mean people who wear gold medals at the Olympics. It can mean people setting new world records. It can mean people who discover cures for something. It can often represent those people reported in the news or history for some outstanding achievement or bravery. Winning often gets associated with those who have already achieved some title or world or national recognition as somebody.

So where does that leave the rest of us? There's no news reporter seeking us out and no national or international recognition. You don't have a famous name and you don't come from a famous family. Sometimes it can be difficult to pursue the win when it might seem "no one knows," "no one's watching," "no one cares," or "I'm not a somebody." Almost feels like winning is not worth pursuing when no one is there patting you on the back, awarding you a medal, or recognizing you in front of your peers.

Winning, then, must be internalized rather than externalized. What we most often view around us is what I call *external winning*. It's the winning and fame of others brought to light by the media, for example, movie stars, political figures, athletes, and heroes. These people's life experiences can deeply impact our own. We can easily learn from them and *bring home* our own adaptation of their process of winning.

When we internalize winning privately, we learn to compete with ourselves in the quiet and solitude of our own potential and capability. We train ourselves to take great pride and personal achievement in those day-to-day successes that only we know we had to dig down deep to pull off. It's every time we *advance the action,* inch by inch if necessary, or *turn on the lights* of wisdom and planning to open new doors of opportunity. It's every time we try something new and develop our sense of adventure and learning. It's every time we accept that not everything we touch turns to gold. It's fighting the good fight. It's knowing when we've done our very best! It's accepting what we can't change and having the courage to change the things we can. It's competing with yourself to better your best. It's following your dreams when you're the only one who wants that dream. It's about knowing who you are. It's about knowing what you want and going after it by removing obstacle after obstacle until you grab that gold ring!

Sometimes we may think that winning happens when life stays nice and calm and gives us the *wiggle room* we need to make it happen. Au contraire, the real challenge is to "win at life when life's not looking." When we go through tough or challenging times, we can be taken down by *life itself.* Then once the difficulty passes, we tend to settle in to normalcy or complacency rather than take advantage of making our move up now that the coast is clear. You know if *difficulty* were a person who knocked on your door, *difficulty* wouldn't phone first to see if you're ready for your next *difficulty.* It just shows up and dumps it on you. Amazingly, most of us tend to adapt and make the best of a bad situation. Why then, when the coast is clear, don't we jump back in the race and go after what we really want rather than sit and wait for more *difficulty* to show up at our door? Once we see that *clear shot,* we ought to go for it while *life's not looking* and difficulty is no longer knocking at our door.

Sister St. Matthew was my high school business teacher. She was the first to teach me to compete with myself in shorthand. I was the fastest in my shorthand class. I had reached 120 words a minute for five minutes, first in my class by April of my senior year in high school. She then worked with me for the remaining time we had toward the 140 words a minute goal. I was into it. I was bettering my best. I was excited about the possibility and pushed myself. I was willing to work extra hours. Now, I didn't happen to reach that goal of 140 words a minute for 5 minutes before graduation, but what I did learn was to compete with myself. She awakened the competitor in me and it's never gone to sleep since. That victory for me was a private one. Only she and I were ever aware of it. She was one of the first people from whom I learned to win internally. Without question in my mind, she was a winner and it rubbed off on me. So let's all pass it on! Sister St. Matthew is in heaven now. I imagine she's passing it on up there too at 140 words a minute!

So go ahead, my friends, look at every single day as your opportunity to win. Look at every single thing you do as your opportunity to better your best. After all, winning is actually easier than losing. Losing is a bummer and winning, while it is work, is definitely more fun and exciting because it keeps our energy and enthusiasm up.

Often when I speak, audiences ask me, "Are you always like this?" My answer is, "No, only when I want to win." But I've discovered that winning is definitely easier than losing, and when *difficulty comes a knockin'*, I'm just not available.

LESSON #13

THE GOOD THE BAD AND THE UGLY

The good the bad and the ugly could define the learning process. Ever felt really bad for yourself? Maybe even embarrassed about things that you've stupidly done or things that have been done to you that you feel you didn't deserve. Do you spend lots of time going over and over why something shouldn't have happened? Are you agonizing and unhappy with the *why* lingering in your brain?

Something that's occurred to me that has been a real sense of consolation is that life teaches you two things: what you want and what you don't want. Almost gives you a reason to thank those who've helped form your convictions that go something like this, "I will never..."

You see we do learn by looking around. We are constantly assessing and accepting or rejecting circumstances every single day that we either add to our *wannabe* list or add to our *never wannabe* list. Everything around us helps us *define* who we are, what we want to represent, and how we want to approach our lives. Fortunately for us as Americans, we have the freedom to pursue what we choose without persecution. Now, that sure beats the opposite by a long shot.

As adults we tend to try to prevent our children from experiencing unnecessary negatives. However, perhaps we ought to consider that negatives are not a bad way to learn at all (barring of course the life threatening). Whether in the home or workplace, let's encourage people to explore their ideas, perhaps coaching to help identify the real goal, the plan, and the expected outcome. And, should failure be the outcome, then let's go back to "what did we learn from it?" as we help that person move on.

We live in a world of "don't do this" and "don't do that." So, how do we deal with our curiosity and natural instincts? One way I've harnessed in my own natural instincts is by asking myself, "What's the worst thing that can happen?" Once I answer that question to myself, then I determine from that perspective whether what I want to try is worth it or not for me. We often hear people say, "I wouldn't do this or that." What needs to be factored in is how important is it to you? We should do what we do or try by first making sure that our intentions are not defiant or revengeful, but rather in honest pursuit of what we believe is in our best interest. We need to be true to ourselves and accept the fact that not everything we touch turns to gold because some of what we touch will simply teach us not to touch again. In our game of winning, the process of elimination helps define the direction we take. Unpleasant things that happen should be incorporated into the fabric of our own success as directional cues. We can then move on successfully while developing a healthy respect for what we learned and where we've been.

Difficulty should be the building block to strength of character, understanding, and humility as we carry the *torch* in our own personal Olympics. Mohammed Ali certainly taught us that lesson when he lit the caldron at the Atlanta Games. While many of us can look back upon personal tragedy and disappointment, it is important to learn from it and move on. If there's rain on your parade, march faster to find the sun. Oh, and by the way, stop some winners along the way and ask if there's a shorter route to get there!

LESSON #14

CHALLENGING THE STATUS QUO

Have you ever looked around and wondered why some people seem to reach heights others only dream of? Have you ever questioned why some people seem to have more luck getting what they want more of the time? Maybe the rationale that follows goes something like, "I'm just not that pushy." One of the things I've observed over the years dealing with thousands of sales people, some very successful and some not so successful, is that the people less successful clearly seemed to give up too soon. It's what I describe as being 8 ½ months pregnant. If you could end the pregnancy two weeks early with no problems, there would be no shortage of takers. In other words, 8 ½ months is about as close as you get to victory with the child bearing over and done with but oh those last two weeks seem absolutely endless. You're the closest to being done that anyone can imagine, but the vulnerability is at its high. Of course in pregnancy, we have no choice but to *stick it out*.

Life, however, is very different. Many factors can create vulnerability that leads to giving up too soon. These factors certainly include fearing failure or embarrassment, being in a hurry, giving up on the goal by telling ourselves it wasn't that important to begin with, having faulty information, taking things too literally, etc. Times like these should be a real red flag to persevere and successfully deal with vulnerability to allow ourselves the opportunity to press on. It's real easy to *tag* someone as stubborn. It's real easy for the person who really doesn't care about your issue. So negativity, internal or external, can play a big role in having you *cave in* to outside pressure while convincing yourself that it's really not that important.   This kind of negativity can come from spouses, children, family members, or best friends. Then, we start second-guessing ourselves.

I remember my kids would laugh anytime I'd try on a hat in a department store. They thought it looked *funny*. To this day I can hear them laughing in my head even if they're not with me anytime I try a hat on. Frankly speaking, this certainly is not a major issue by any standard. Hats on women really are not that popular. But let's say the issue is really something important to you. The people closest to us can be the same people who dismantle our dreams.

I can remember in my late 20s when I had become pretty successful as a nationally recognized sales manager and had a solid business up and running for myself. I still had two pre-school children and a house to run, so I entertained the idea of getting a housekeeper for myself. Now mind you, no one I knew had a housekeeper. So when I put the word out to people I knew that I was looking for a housekeeper once a week for about four hours, the reaction was interesting. Reactions included "Why don't you just stay home and take care of your kids like you're supposed to." "Why don't you stop killing yourself?" and "Exactly who do you think you are?" The truth was that I didn't feel like I was killing myself. As a matter of fact I was having the time of my life. But as I thought about what was important to me at that point in my career, I realized that I wanted quality family time on weekends rather than a long list of chores. I guess I knew deep down that it was the best way for me to "cope" with the challenges I faced with a young family and a career in the '70s. You know I did find a housekeeper (no thanks or help to my acquaintances) and as time went on, I came to realize that it was the right decision for me despite the raised eyebrows. I didn't realize it but I was really learning to challenge status quo. Admittedly, I did feel a little funny about getting a housekeeper but it took very little time to get over it. I've had a housekeeper ever since and I would highly recommend it in a two-career household.

We all go through times where we have difficulty separating what we truly want or need from popular opinion of family, friends, area, workplace, or general pecking order. I think we need to take all opinions, weigh them, and dig down for the courage to *challenge the status quo* by being true to ourselves and our goals. Don't ever let anyone rain on your parade, even if you're the only one in the parade.

I remember one time not too long ago, I had received a flyer in the mail about an area rug I wanted very much. The store was to have them for only 10 days on a special event promotion. I saved the flyer, made sure I arrived early on day one, and began my search for this rug. Having walked around the store with no success finding it, I went to Customer Service and asked where the area rugs on special were. The person kind of gave me the *brush-off.* I got the feeling she took a guess at where she sent me to look for the rug. Still not locating the item, I returned to Customer Service a second time and she then suggested I come back every couple of days to see if they were out. Needless to say, that definitely was a useless option to me. As a matter of fact, her suggestion worked just the opposite. I was now on an absolute mission to track this rug down. Now, right about that time, my very patient husband said, "You know you might have to start reciting the Serenity Prayer" (you know the one about God grant me the courage and wisdom). Again, the reverse effect occurred. I spotted a manager station so I ran the scenario by the manager and he agreed to walk with me in my search. Again, we came up dry but he kindly offered to give me his business card and told me to call him after his forklift people came in. He assured me they knew where everything was. I guess at that point, I felt I had exhausted all possibilities with the employees in the store. But, I decided on one more walk through before I started reciting my Serenity Prayer. And, wouldn't you know it, this time I discovered a large box that was only partially open. Lo and behold, there was my rug. The *fly in the ointment* was that you had to come upon this box from a certain direction to get a glimpse of the rug color. I can't tell you how thrilled I was to snag my purchase. They could have tripled the price and I think I'd still have bought it. It's crazy little times like that when you're reminded of the fact that there's probably no one who cares more about what you want/need than you.

My best advice is to *question, question, and requestion* because many people won't be honest enough to tell you they're winging it and really don't know. The truth is YOU ARE on your own. Be willing to discover, search, question, and double check so that if you do need to start reciting your Serenity Prayer, you will know that you were willing to *challenge the status quo* and that your goal really was not realistic at that time. Accept the fact that discovery and popular opinion will probably always be part of the challenge.

When I was growing up, parents of Down's syndrome babies were frequently advised to institutionalize them. It was only with the courage of those parents who were willing to *challenge the status quo* and give their children as normal an upbringing as they could, that we learned how much potential these children have. Only then came the discoveries of how capable these special children are. Their treasure chest of potential was opened by people like you and me who chose not to institutionalize their children. It took a lot of courage to challenge status quo.

So feel good about having the courage to say, "What if?" Why not explore different options? Discovery is what teaches us to be innovative and creative. Progress couldn't exist without it. And remember, there IS a difference between being stubborn and persistent. Stubborn can be digging in *without being logical*. Persistence can be digging in *logically*. So go ahead and be persistent and keep your eyes on your goal! If you need to don't be afraid to challenge status quo.

LESSON #15

EXCELLENCE IS LIKE
A DUMP TRUCK IN YOUR DRIVEWAY

Excellence is an interesting word. Whenever I do corporate training programs, this word often brings snickering from the crowd, especially when management wrote the mission statement and tossed in the word excellence. What I've learned is that excellence is not perfection. I'm not so sure perfection exists. But I've certainly wondered if the snickering audiences really represent the perception of bosses in their ivory towers shooting for perfection, while the folks in the trenches are feeling defeated before they try.

I've come to realize that excellence represents the standards we *shoot for*. I've always told my audiences that if you don't shoot for excellence, then exactly what do you shoot for? It might be hard to believe that if you ask people for nothing, you can actually get less than nothing. So what are you shooting for then? *Is it getting behind, getting by, or getting ahead?*

High performance standards are there to challenge us to compete with ourselves or others. If we don't shoot to stretch, then we won't achieve at the highest level we're capable of.

Picture yourself cleaning out your residence for the millionth time, and rather apathetic about the task. When the rug rats arrive on a rainy and muddy day, you stand at the door like the kitchen police warning them about trying to keep the place ship-shape for at least an hour. All the while, you're telling yourself that cleaning is useless anyway. Now imagine yourself shoveling dirt out of your residence, while there's a dump truck in your driveway with a crew that is *shoveling it in* at the same time you're *shoveling it out*. You'll love this. You see excellence is <u>not</u> perfection. It's simply shoveling faster than *they* do. Now, just imagine that the dump truck represents *progress.* You see, excellence is staying ahead of the curve by challenging ourselves to beat the odds. Personal achievement is directly tied to bettering our best and not being whipped or taken down by simple everyday tasks or tough challenges.

While perfection may feel impossible, meeting high standards is not impossible. So, go ahead, shoot for the stars and never be embarrassed to shoot for excellence. It's one way we can distinguish ourselves from the average bear. A healthy understanding of what excellence represents is what we want to pass on to our children and their children. So as of now, let's have a few less people snickering over the word excellence!

LESSON #16

ARE YOU A VICTIM OF CIRCUMSTANCES OR A VICTOR OVER CIRCUMSTANCES?

Are you a victim of circumstances or a victor over circumstances? Truth is we certainly can't completely prevent unforeseen circumstances from catching us off guard from time to time. Many lessons in this book can help us stack the odds in our favor to reduce needless struggle. This lesson is about the understanding we need to cultivate when we are taken down by frustration or difficulty, whether we do it to ourselves or it's caused by outside influences.

It certainly is very natural to feel bad for ourselves given a negative we don't feel we deserved. And, by the way, Murphy's Law is alive and well. However, once we recognize these all too human feelings, it's important that you give your brain a chance to kick in. Christopher Reeve, who played Superman, certainly has become a tremendous role model and example of how to become a victor over circumstances by devoting his life to championing hope and a cure for spinal cord injuries. I must admit it's hard to imagine what possible solution could reverse this difficult circumstance. However, Christopher Reeve has become a pioneer in helping more of us *believe in possibility* regarding spinal cord injuries. Hard to imagine as it is, I must admit I've begun hoping along with him that this impossible dream comes true. Frankly, I still can't figure out how a plane gets off the ground much less how they got to the moon, so I suppose anything is possible with focus and commitment.

I guess if we relate this example to our everyday comings and goings, we can apply some of what other winners have done successfully. Some lessons to be learned begin with assessing the situation, getting information from other people facing those circumstances, finding who among them is dealing most successfully with their circumstances, focusing on solutions to advance the action, committing ourselves to discovery rather than grief, and helping others.

A wonderful example that comes to mind is Al-Anon, which is a support group devoted to educating and helping the families of alcoholics deal more successfully with the challenge of alcoholism. This is where education begins. Here's where you get the pointers that may elude the family and shed some hope and light on a dismal set of circumstances. Al-Anon is not there to solve your problems, but it is there to help you sift and sort toward a better solution for you. It helps provide some control in what appears to be uncontrollable.

Beware of the *woe is me* victim mentality. Unfortunate circumstances must be viewed as your opportunity to be a hero. Here we go again and not exactly the time when we feel like being heroes. Focus your talent and potential on the resolve to find the best ways to deal with the circumstances you're facing.

My speaking career was born from challenging circumstances. Business can be wonderful but sometimes overnight it's just not wonderful anymore. I've seen so many people face very challenging career problems, many of which can be just bigger than we are. They can be situations that truly are beyond our control at the time. Not fair? Sure, I understand. But the question is, how can you land on your feet? When I personally made the transition to my speaking career, I had to refocus my efforts in a new direction. Speaking was always a passion for me as was the idea of helping other people. I was committed to using my talent and winner skills to successfully reinvent myself.

Sadly, as I think about the people I've observed facing challenging circumstances, too many became victims and too few became victors. Believing in possibility and not allowing yourself to sink into less than you want to be will be the inspiration that allows for the strength of character and hero within you to emerge.

Hopefully, we use our everyday disappointments as our training ground and springboard for the tougher challenges that will be thrown at us during the Game of Life. So, come on, pick yourself up and dust yourself off. Tell yourself that if *life* attempts to lower the bar on you, it becomes your time to fight back and develop your resolve. Get that bar back where you want it to be so you too can join the ranks of those who have become a victor over circumstances!

LESSON #17

ARE YOU MOVING THE CRITICAL MASS?

I love this one. My husband and I have had many discussions on this. This lesson gets us thinking about the struggle versus coasting dilemma we sometimes face.

Moving the critical mass can be summed up in learning to do something *enough* that we develop a comfort level of confidence and skill. Being uncomfortable doing anything can really be a symptom of a lack of skill, confidence, knowledge, or technique in achieving that comfort level that makes all the difference.

I remember when I started traveling all over the country doing full-day seminars back in 1993. I was traveling to about 80 to 100 cities a year. It occurred to me that this would be a great way to become a national speaker and gain exposure to companies far and wide across this country. My goal was to do four days a month. However, next thing I knew I was booked six months in advance for eight to ten days a month. Part of me knew this would be a wonderful opportunity to advance my speaking career but this commitment was a real stretch from my original idea of four days a month.

What I did then was apply this lesson of moving the critical mass by telling myself that I would extend myself these additional days by getting better faster and getting rid of the butterflies sooner. Incidentally what I discovered, to my surprise, was that I adapted to travel much better than I ever expected. I was able to maintain this commitment of eight to ten days a month for six years not just six months. This commitment allowed me the opportunity to stretch my speaking career further than I ever would have dreamed possible.

Any time we embark on a *stretch*, we create that crash course that helps us get confident and comfortable sooner. Sure, it's a trade-off, but a trade-off that's well worth it. It occurs to me that struggle is not fun, so why not get over it as quickly as you can and get to the good part.

The lesson to be learned is to do enough of something to move that critical mass. Nothing is worse than doing something for the first time. So why on earth would we continue to put ourselves in that position? This also helps explain why the people at the top seem to do what they do with more ease than those struggling at the bottom. They've figured out that *winning breeds winning.* So I guess that also means that *not winning breeds more struggle.* When you look at it this way, it makes a lot of sense.

Now picture an incline. Doing too little is like inching your way up that incline. It certainly feels like a struggle and perhaps enough of a struggle to give up or give in. Sometimes we just don't do enough of something to ever develop a good skill level. We're half in and half out at the same time. However, imagine getting yourself to a point where the incline is behind you and now your efforts begin to pay off. I guess that helps explain the word *transition*. Any time you want to excel at something, you've got to consider *moving the critical mass.* Reach a point where you are indeed up and running and it feels like you can keep it going. It's the part of personal achievement that is truly exhilarating.

Training and speaking provide good examples of this. It's not uncommon to hear people comment on having had training in the past or, "I've heard that before," as if once is enough. Guess what? Hearing it 10 years ago doesn't mean you're any good at it. It doesn't even mean you can apply the information. Developing skill comes from knowledge, practice, repetition, and more knowledge. Pretty soon the information becomes natural and easy to apply. The more we study something, the more we help it become a natural part of us and the more likely we add it to who we are or who we want to become.

Moving the critical mass is the *monomaniac* part of commitment. It takes what we do to a higher level of expertise and removes all obstacles and distraction to maintain focus.

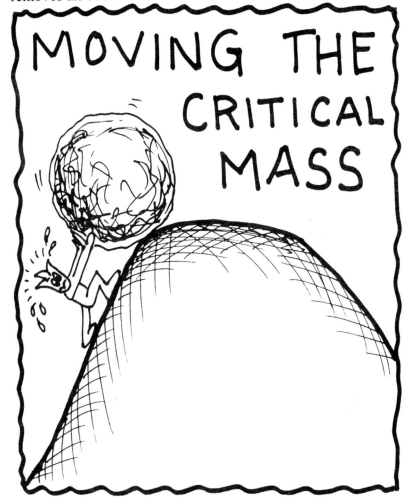

LESSON #18

CHANGING THE COURSE OF HISTORY

Okay, here's where we work on courage. In *The Wizard of Oz*, the lion went to Oz hoping to find courage. It's easy to think that lions automatically have courage. So what happened to the wimpy lion in *The Wizard of Oz*? Perhaps, the lion had courage to those of us who aren't lions, but maybe in the lion population, this lion realized how *many* lions around him had more courage than he did. I guess it can be somewhat disconcerting looking around and feeling like you don't measure up to your surroundings or what's around you.

While most of us probably won't take a magical trip to *Oz* anytime soon or win the lottery, we certainly owe ourselves an opportunity to *advance the action* to reach the goal or dream that's really important to us. Perhaps you lived in an environment where you *learned* you could be anything you wanted to be. Not everyone has learned that, in part because when you dare to leave the environment you're in, the people around you may become painfully aware that you could be on to something that has eluded them. You now become something of an oddity in their perception.

It's not uncommon to hear things like, "Oh, you don't need to do that!" "Why can't you just be happy with what you have?" "Chill." "Quit killing yourself." Daring to venture too far from the *known* can be an unpopular position. Sometimes you might be the only person who wants what you want as badly as you do. It'll take *courage* to face those closest to you and patiently solicit their support for you and your dreams. You see, pioneering can be seen as ridiculous and not terribly different than when Christopher Columbus set sail. Imagine how wacky that was perceived when it was strongly believed that the world was flat.

There's a book written in the '80s that illustrates *pioneering* so well. It was called *Jonathan Livingston Seagull*. In the story Jonathan, the seagull, was unhappy just being the average seagull scavenging for food all day. He dreamed of learning to soar and fly like no other seagull had ever done. So off he went, alone and lonely, to see what he could discover and achieve. What he discovered was the exhilaration of personal achievement. He was changing the course of history for all seagulls. Along the way, though, he discovered that he had been looked down on by his peers and ostracized for his approach. The other seagulls perceived Jonathan's adventure as turning his back on them and their ways. Why couldn't he be satisfied just being a seagull like everyone else? It was only when history began to emerge with the next generation of seagulls that Jonathan received validation. The next generation saw him as a hero among seagulls and they longed for his insight and technique.

You see, *the known* is such a comfort zone for people, and *the unknown* represents a place of uncertainty, danger, and failure by those who have not yet come to embrace a *new known*. You *can* dare to be different and unique as you learn to distinguish yourself from the masses and change the course of history for yourself and your family.

For me, it was a mission from my early twenties to change the course of history. It was my mission to pull myself out of the *ends meet* mentality and work hard to take advantage of the marvelous opportunity that this wonderful country affords everyone. I wanted to erase the mystery of "where do people get the money?" I wanted college and opportunity (which never come free) to be part of my children's *known*. It certainly wasn't part of my *known*.

We all begin with some set of circumstances, some of which we like and perhaps some we'd like to change. Know in your heart what was good about your circumstances, know clearly what you'd like to change, and set out like Christopher Columbus to discover it. You can't get to second base without taking your foot off first base. Understand that resistance is part of leaving the *known*. Be brave enough to follow your dream. Changing the course of history is always within your grasp when you believe and understand that in your own heart and mind!

LESSON #19

DISCOVER YOUR OWN TREASURE CHEST

Have you ever heard how we all have more potential than we could ever possibly use? I certainly remember in my younger years thinking to myself, "Could that *possibly* be true?" After all, how could we even begin to know how much of what we have we have already used up, how much we have left, or how much is a lot? Do we even have as much as others? Sometimes it might not feel like we do.

I like to use the example of our potential being like a wonderful *treasure chest*. Picture it as the most prized and beautiful possession you own. But like anything we get *used to* owning, sometimes we can forget just how gorgeous ours really is. Remember no one else on earth has a treasure chest exactly like yours. Yours is uniquely yours and quite possibly the envy of others. Others may say, "Boy, he's really good at that. If only I were as good at that."

Often we spend way too much time checking out other people's treasure chests, comparing them to ours, and using that knowledge to downgrade the beauty and value of our own treasure chest. And, even worse, some people spend so much time admiring the treasure chests of others that they have relegated themselves to using their treasure chest as a *bench* to sit on, dreaming of "what if." All the while, we forget what's inside our own. As a matter of fact, we haven't used it in so long it starts to look and feel old, outdated, and no longer useful.

You owe it to yourself to be very aware that your *own* potential holds the key to making a better life for you, instead of expecting someone else to do it. While we can learn from others, we must harness that learning and be sure it doesn't become envy. We have the responsibility to take whatever knowledge and experience we discover from others and make it uniquely ours.

We shouldn't try to copy other people, but rather take the best of what we discover and convert it to our own uniqueness, like discovering a new color to add to our masterpiece. Always remember you have a beautiful treasure chest. It's everything you need for your own unique success story. Respect your potential, use it, be true to yourself, and be proud of the uniqueness that is you. We can dare to be different without alienating ourselves from the masses. It all comes from recognizing clearly what is in your own best interest and what you want to achieve with your talent and potential. So, go ahead. Check your treasure chest every day. You'll be amazed at what it holds to create your own masterpiece. Oh, sometimes you might have to dig a little. Don't expect the contents to jump out at you just because you lift the cover! Just remember to keep on digging for that winning combination!

LESSON #20

IT'S LONELY AT THE TOP

While most of us have heard this saying, I'm wondering how many can really relate to the feeling of being out front, setting the standard, and being applauded, while at the same time being critiqued, jeered, or snickered at.

In Lesson #19 we talked about those folks who are sitting on their treasure chests and becoming envious of the treasure chests of others. It's almost incomprehensible that someone could be the leader, expert, and standard-bearer, yet still come under fire by people who have never achieved at the same level.

Evidence of this phenomenon has never been clearer than after the events of 9/11 when our country came under attack by terrorists. How shocked we are to learn how many people just plain hate Americans and freedom. Seems unfair because we work to build a better life. We don't fight with or invade our neighbors. We give to many other countries and we even help countries we're not particularly thrilled with. We stand for freedom and justice. Sad as it may be, our success can be the envy of others.

There's always the question of just how much we should extend ourselves to others. History has proven that if we don't spread the good word then the bad word gets out. Holding out a helping hand can sometimes be the only means to tear down negative perceptions and create a sense of eye opening and reciprocity. When people see clearly for themselves without the tainted image of second-hand and third-hand perception, it is only then that we begin to tear down walls.

Applying this lesson to everyday life can mean that we develop a certain tolerance for the misperceptions of others and understand unfairness is real, yet doing the right thing is a first step to embracing those who would hurt us. This can apply in the family or workplace as well as between nations. With just intentions and good planning, we must believe goodness and justice will prevail.

The leader clearly bears the responsibility to make things right. And we're all leaders. *Lonely at the top* can be cured by helping others *up* alongside us, one at a time, until the standard becomes set and others see the vision and opportunity that can become their own. Sitting at the top and minding our own business is not an option. Helping others *up with us* is!

LESSON #21

ARE YOU MINIMIZING OR MAXIMIZING?

This lesson has just hit me recently as I observe audiences and people I've come in contact with. It occurs to me that not everyone spends time in pursuit of the win to improve the status quo. You see, shooting for the best is the only option there is unless you truly don't care about something. Of course, that would indicate some kind of conscious or unconscious decision on the part of the individual.

Consider how you perceive yourself personally or professionally as part of your world. We are what we think, therefore, if we start to think bigger, we can achieve a greater measure of success. I remember, early in my career, hearing people I respected make the comment, "They just don't think big enough." Hearing that statement raised the question, "How do you learn to think bigger than you currently do?"

Over the years of developing winner thinking, I've discovered an interesting phenomenon about people. I'm not sure people realize it, but you'll hear people say something like, "Well I'm better than so and so" or "So and so is *really* bad." It makes me wonder how we see ourselves? As we look around our world, are we looking *down* to find people we're better than or are we looking *up* to see how we compare with the best there is?

I call it *minimizing* or *maximizing*. Small thinking would be demonstrated by scraping the bottom of the barrel in our own self-assessment. Big thinking would be demonstrated by the curiosity to learn and discover what it is we haven't yet figured out that others at the top have figured out. It's a healthy approach to growth rather than fear or envy. It represents how we see ourselves and how we set our standards both personally and professionally.

In the workplace, it's almost perceived as idiotic to dare to be different. The pressure in the workplace to be an *average bear,* rather than a standard bearer, can be difficult. Once again, courage creeps in as we respect others around us but never let it deter us from being the best at whatever we choose. It should be a lesson we pass on. But, as adults, are we courageous enough to be true to ourselves? It's what we ask our kids to do in high school when we tell them to *just say no* to peer pressure.

Sadly, the workplace is filled with complacency, for example, the "It's not my job" and "I'm only" mentality. Complacency is a clear sign of *minimizing* in our surroundings and building our own glass ceiling. In effect, we are stunting our own growth potential. Why not dare enough to look up at the best and ask ourselves, "How do they do what they do?" "What part of their success can I extract and use for my own success?" Are we really being true to ourselves and our potential when we try to do as little as possible to get by? Are we embracing potential and possibility to build our own winner thinking? Incidentally, here's a tip for the workplace: employees tend to gauge how good they are by listing the *who's who* of people worse than themselves. Bosses, on the other hand, gauge employees by the best employee. Therein lies a real problem when employees and bosses use *different* standards to determine employee value to the organization.

The answer has been very clear to me over recent years. Engaging in *minimizing* thinking will always work against you. Engaging in *maximizing* thinking as you hook your wagon to a star will always carry you further in your quest for success. It's what you shoot for that determines how small or big a thinker you really are. Thinking big will always make for a more positive existence when it comes to standards of excellence and high expectations for yourself. Be the best and expect the best always!

LESSON #22

I DON'T KNOW WHAT I DON'T KNOW

When we started being curious about the facts of life growing up, one friend's parents were a little more forthcoming with information than many at that time. While I tell you they were more forthcoming, make no mistake, there was never a flow of information as *thought starters* for us. As a matter of fact, I remember one day, my friend's mother telling my friend and me that we could ask them anything we wanted to ask them. Now, while I thought this was the best offer I'd heard so far, I still remember feeling rather desperate at not even knowing what I didn't know. I'd have loved to ask questions, if only I knew what questions to ask.

I was in complete disbelief the first time my older cousin let me *in* on the fact that my mother had a baby in her stomach. I wondered, "Could that possibly be how it works?" I then posed the question to an aunt, who happened to be a nurse. She reassured me that babies were delivered to the hospital and then the mothers went to pick them up. Whew! What a relief! Of course, I now realize how naïve I was growing up because people during that time made a regular practice of withholding information.

I guess there comes a time when we have to care enough about people to just level with them. From my perspective, keeping people in the dark when answers are available is a shame. I guess we first have to care enough about people to help put the *lights on,* as well as believe in them to use the information to improve themselves. Oh, and incidentally, people don't always accept information the first time they hear it, which is where repetition comes in to play.

Very often I hear people make the comment, "Isn't it all just common sense?" Well, the answer is NO. It's only common sense if you've heard it before. If we've been fortunate enough to have learned all we need to know from our parents, teachers, bosses, coworkers, and friends, then yes, we have acquired all "common sense." The truth is there is SO MUCH we could learn from what others know and that knowledge will reduce our struggle and improve the quality of our lives.

For those of us hungry for acquiring good information, as I always have been, we do indeed have the responsibility to spread it around rather than be impatient and disgruntled at those who come up deficient. It's part of the reason I'm writing this book, because I so value the wonderful lessons I've been able to learn from so many. I shudder to think of where I would be if I'd missed any of these lessons.

So, let's not wait for people to approach us, let us be forthcoming and try to spread good wisdom and ideas to others. Let's not just quietly walk into eternity with all our good information tucked under our arm, while critiquing those who haven't yet acquired it.

An idea I highly recommend that has worked well for me over the years is to have a roster of champions or mentors with whom you can discuss, learn, and grow as you navigate your way through stumbling blocks. Help yourself stretch your own thinking by getting input from those people you highly respect who can be objective and forthcoming without judging you. I can think of so many people over the last 35 years who have been in the role of champion for me. They are the people with whom I can be honest without fear of feeling stupid. They are the people I can count on for non-judgmental input as I struggle to clear away a murky picture. Too often we depend too much on ourselves without reaching out to others.

Trust people enough to reach out and up when something is eluding you, especially when you don't know what you don't know, you can't figure out what the missing puzzle piece happens to be, or you have difficulty seeing solutions. Sometimes just knowing you're not alone in your thoughts can be a great source of consolation.

LESSON #23

TWO MYTHS

You know, it's funny how we acquire our perception of how things ought to be. Remember hearing that if you made faces, your face just might stay like that some day? And, wouldn't you be sorry then?

One myth I remember was the one about people who had money had problems. Therefore, having less made life easier. That was pretty believable, especially as a young person, because the message was that simple is better and uncomplicated is the way to go. Sadly, along with that message was the clear implication, "We can't afford that," which meant it was not an option. What the message fosters implicitly is that we should be satisfied and not rock the boat. "What we have is fine." "It'll do." "We don't have much, but we eat good." Is it any wonder why we might be fatter than we should be? When you're taught from day one that food three times a day is a highlight you ought to be thankful for, I'd say the bar has been lowered to the lowest possible rung. People who set goals too low may have some difficulty setting higher ones because fear of failure rocks their boat.

What I've discovered is that when I'm excited about something I'm pursuing, like writing this book, all of a sudden food has less meaning to me because I'm shifting my focus to something new and novel that keeps me at this computer writing this book.

While I think there's certainly a valid message in keeping things simple, I think there is also validity in *rocking our own boat* periodically to see what we're made of. There's validity in challenging the status quo. It's perfectly okay to question whether something can be better and to shoot for it even if others see it as unnecessary.

Another myth is that shooting for goals can just be disappointing anyway and rather than disappoint or embarrass yourself, why not just forego that goal setting idea and "See what happens" or "If it's meant to be, it's meant to be." I often hear people say about goal setting, "What if I don't make it?" It's a common question that illustrates just how people feel deep down about goal setting. The primary focus seems to be that reaching the goal is the only possible outcome that won't embarrass anyone. Even telling someone else about a goal can be difficult. How would I possibly explain myself if it didn't work out?

Truth is that even proactive high achievers don't get a straight shot to success. Frankly, no one gets that regardless of rank or salary. But people who have tossed this myth overboard have come to realize that if they don't reach the goal on the first try, they are prepared to try again. Embarrassment doesn't enter into it. What enters into it is how to approach the goal given the research provided by the first attempt.

We should never be ashamed of missing a goal, if we truly gave it our best. It takes a real winner to explain to subordinates in the workplace or children at home just how the experience affects the pursuit of the goal. We should be ready and willing to share experiences with others. When we do, what we really share is problem solving, commitment, and hope in achieving the results desired. We should focus on how we can inspire others by *pulling the rabbit out of the hat* and help people see that goals can be reached even though it takes numerous attempts.

So, hopefully, we can lay to rest the two myths that can be real roadblocks to success. The first is don't always keep things simple and be willing to take risks to better your position in life. The second is there is no embarrassment in goal setting when you are prepared to move from Plan A to Plan B to Plan C if necessary. Believe in your own ability and potential to figure it out as you go. Let's face it, it's how we enter a marriage and raise kids. Most of us do pretty well figuring as we go, so let's embrace possibility thinking and goal setting as part of our winning masterpiece.

LESSON #24

WHAT IS MOTIVATION?

You know it's been said that motivational speakers are just about hip-hip-hooray, after which we all go back to our bad habits cheering rah-rah-team! You know part of the reason I became a motivational speaker was because of the fabulous speakers I was exposed to throughout my career. They included some familiar and less familiar names: Zig Ziglar, Denis Waitley, Leo Buscaglia, Tom Peters, Dr. Jarvis, Rosita Perez, Jeanne Robertson, Helene Phifer, and Eleanor Gengler, to name a few.

I beg to differ with the rather flimsy explanation of motivation and motivational speakers that permeates. I can still clearly remember the messages delivered by the speakers I've mentioned. They all inspired me. They had a tremendous impact on how I view the world and how I choose to participate in the world. Each and every one was like a *live book* that was animated and full of humor, insight, and a fresh perspective.

Looking back over many of the decisions I've made during my last 35 years, it occurs to me that each and every decision, idea, and application came from motivation. It was some motive, from some speaker somewhere, that helped me go in a new direction, deal better with a particular situation, or gain a deeper understanding of myself and the world around me. And, by the way, I particularly enjoyed being entertained at the same time.

Motivation is about knowledge with impact that sticks to your gut. It helps you find your way through life's maze.

Motivation is the reason why we do what we do every day we live and breathe. Motivation keeps us energized and enthused. It protects attitude, turns on creativity and innovation, and generally helps us hang in there or challenge the status quo.

You know I'm not real fussy where I get my motivation. It could be from a great news story, appreciating someone else's success, observing the winners around me, or from a wonderful motivational speaker. Whatever makes me *think* and makes me *reassess* who I am, where I'm going, and why I'm doing it, is always welcome. I believe in the fact that we don't have to reinvent the wheel. Someone, somewhere, has taken life experience or expertise and put it together in a great program with high impact delivery. I can take it, leave it, or use it if I choose to.

Simply put, motives are reasons why we do what we do. In order to function at the highest level, motives will certainly get fine-tuned as we go. Motives that go from "three squares a day and a roof over your head" to motives that can change history can inspire us all. Working to make *ends meet* can be a painful and difficult motive. Making a difference in this world can make what we do meaningful. Every so often, we can lose our way, but motives bring us back. Hopefully, we don't just wait for that usually painful *wake up call*!

LESSON #25

BY BEING PUSHED, I GREW FAST

In a recent interview I heard with Colin Powell, Secretary of State, he recalled his experience growing up in a black family in the Bronx. At that time, the challenges for African-Americans were tremendous. Yet, Colin Powell recalled the marvelous family values that were instilled in him to reach for the stars and not let anything get in his way. He recalled getting his education and joining the Armed Forces, where he was quickly promoted and recognized for his leadership. He pointed out, "by being pushed, I grew fast."

I wonder how we view *being pushed* or *pushing ourselves*? You know the world will tell you to "quit killing yourself" all the while you start to reconsider the value of what you do. Sometimes others, aside from family and friends, see more in us than we see in ourselves. Frequently we talk ourselves down from or second guess ideas that seem too lofty.

Several years ago, I can remember meeting a pediatrician who had a delightful personality. We got talking about success and challenges and he mentioned to me that when he took his SATs to get into college he hadn't scored high enough to get in. With a fun laugh he said, "I discovered that SAT stood for 'sorry about that'." The world around us can easily tell us we can or can't do something, but in this instance, Dr. Brown decided to push himself and successfully reached his dream of becoming a pediatrician.

Sometimes the pushing can come from outside, like Colin Powell received from his family and his promotions in the Armed Forces. Sometimes pushing comes from within, like it did with Dr. Brown.

I remember early in my speaking career when I decided to work with some corporate training companies, I had contacted several seminar companies and sent in my demo video. It was the first time in my speaking career I had pushed myself to a higher level. That first attempt was a rejection from one of them. I got a very professional letter that told me that my style was not what they were looking for. I kept that letter because I knew they were wrong. I remember thinking, "If you don't need speakers, then say you don't need speakers." Then came the call from the next company, Dun & Bradstreet Business Education Services, which was absolutely delighted with my video. That phone call resulted in a six year stint that propelled me into their top rank of in-demand speakers. What a wonderful working relationship I had with them. That connection lead to an even more prestigious association for me on the faculty of the American Management Association in Times Square in New York. So often, we let the wrong people or situations become *our yardstick* to validate who we are or who we aspire to be. Without *great* past training and confidence, I'm not sure I would have survived that rejection.

You see we all get rejection at some time. It is at that time especially that we need to push ourselves, refocus, and take a roundabout route, if necessary, to get where we want to be. Doors may be open, but if they're closed for you, check a window and hoist yourself in! If the world doesn't discover you or push you, then push yourself.

LESSON #26

THE RULES OF WINNING

1. <u>Hang out with winners</u>. Whiners, complainers, and negative people don't qualify. Ever notice when you're out with a couple that nag and nit-pick? Pretty soon you're nagging and nit-picking along with them. However, if you're out with friends who are just dating or newlyweds still in the *touchy-feely stage*, you find yourselves behaving more *touchy-feely* than you would in the company of *nit-pickers*. The same standard applies in the workplace. Misery loves company and it's easy to fall right into that pattern. Winners are too busy problem solving to waste their time here.

2. <u>Be a quick study</u>. When you discover something that obviously works, apply it immediately. Nothing's more exciting than seeing immediate results while the emotion of the moment exists. So many people lack the success others achieve because they never get around to making it happen. I look at it like a new outfit someone gives me for free. All I have to do is put it on. Application is a key to making it happen!

3. <u>Practice, repeat, practice</u>. Make new habits *live for you* by making them comfortable as quickly as you can. Practice enough to stack the odds in your favor.

4. <u>Be unique and be true to yourself</u>. Be smart enough to take the best of what you see and personalize it to yourself. *Your application* of an idea can make it work even better for you.

5. <u>Continue to challenge yourself</u>. Emeril says it best: "Kick it up a notch." Always be on the lookout for making something better, best, great, or outstanding.

6. <u>Catch winning everywhere you can</u>. Observe people around you and analyze what makes them successful. Learn how they think and perform. Catch their passion and pick their brains.

7. <u>Get rid of bad habits</u>. Those things that get you nowhere like complacency, procrastination, lack of goal setting, or following the crowd.

8. <u>Develop winning habits</u>. Perseverance, commitment, goal setting, and self-discipline set you apart from the average bear. Take risks to stretch out of your comfort zone.

9. <u>Become a proactive high achiever</u>. The good news is that this group definitely doesn't *whine*. They *plan* for success and get behind it with a passion to make it happen. No pity parties here. These people could fall into a mud puddle and come up wearing a new suit.

10. <u>Be an obstacle remover</u>. Here is where the rubber meets the road. It is cleverness, creativity, and innovation coming into play. The sheer excitement of *pulling a rabbit out of the hat* is like magic, personal magic!

IF YOU *BELIEVE* IN MAGIC,
COME ALONG WITH ME!

LESSON #27

IT'S NOT WHERE YOU START,
IT'S WHERE YOU FINISH

This phrase is one of my favorites. Of course it feels like it was written for me exclusively. In reality, it's a song from the musical *See Saw* starring Tommy Tune and Michele Lee in the '70s. So often we have the mistaken notion that things should sort of line up for us in order to proceed effectively. However, so many successful people started businesses in their garages before building their empire. Actors and actresses often live from hand-to-mouth until they break through to stardom. So many have told of the odd jobs they've done just to get by in the pursuit of their dreams.

We don't exactly get great consolation from those people who say they were walking down the street or sitting in a restaurant and someone of distinction discovers them. I'm convinced stories like these get told because they are very *rare* circumstances. But, somehow, the rest of us still yearn for someone to help make our own pursuit of success easier.

Wouldn't we all love a hero to rescue and discover us? Look at all the people Oprah has helped become successful. Ever thought to yourself, "What about me?" People in my audiences ask me all the time if I ever see myself on "Oprah." My answer is, "No, not really." Sometimes I feel like my response almost doesn't match my goals, but actually I guess, in reality, I just never expect someone else to make me successful. I guess I've stopped expecting success to come from anywhere but myself. I've learned to depend on myself and put one foot in front of the other every day.

When I started as a professional speaker, there were very few who saw what I saw as a great idea. Au contraire, it was more like, "Who's going to pay you?" I remember thinking, "I haven't figured that out yet." I knew that my husband, my children, and a few friends were the only people who thought this was a winner for me.

Breaks? Don't make the mistake of waiting for them. Take advantage if they get here, but in the meantime, be plotting your course. It was always interesting to me to hear young people say they wanted to earn $100,000 year and drive a Porsche. While many of us might never try for such a *pie in the sky* dream, everyone has the right to set their sights and make it happen. There are no prerequisites other than learning to win! Having nothing to start with should never discourage us from learning, pursuing, and making it happen. It's important that we don't allow poverty or misfortune to exclude us from setting whatever goals we want to shoot for. History has countless people who beat the odds to create success.

I have learned that no matter where you come from or what you have, it's not where you start it's where you finish that's important. And the finish line is there for everyone.

LESSON #28

CLIMBING THE LADDER OF SUCCESS

A true measure of success is our ability to share success with others. Good leaders are good teachers and good teachers are good leaders. Like in the story of Jonathan Livingston Seagull, Jonathan found true success when he was able to share it with others. It's the validation of our achievement by others. It's the legacy we leave behind. It's the ladder we build upon which others may climb. It's our ability to put a fresh set of footprints in the snow and make the way easier for others. It's the clues we leave behind in our wake that give others hope. It's what we leave our children in *what to shoot for* and how to *pass along success* generation after generation.

When we arrive at the pearly gates and get asked what we did with our potential, hopefully the answer is not "loitering." One time I was doing a program and was asking the audience what they were personally excited about. One woman said, "Retiring." I said, "Really, when are you retiring?" She said, "Fifteen years." Imagine loitering your life away waiting for something like that? This person's functioning completely depended on retiring. It's kind of a sad scenario. And the fault lies in her own outlook, whether she realizes it or not.

I'm a firm believer that we always want to continue our *climb* up the ladder of success. We have so much opportunity available to us in this country. We are truly the privileged. I always figured if I could be somewhat successful in my first 25 years when I knew nothing, imagine how successful I could be if I just pay attention for the rest of the time. The sky is the limit! We need to keep reaching for that next rung on our ladder of success.

There are more and more people in their 40s, 50s, 60s, and 70s who are on computers. They are leading the way and are an inspiration to the rest. They didn't stop climbing just because they didn't grow up with it. It's not where you start, it's where you finish. I say get yourself a guru and get going. You probably won't have to look any further than your grandchildren for help. Being older or unfamiliar shouldn't be an excuse! We all have the responsibility to remain progressive role models as long as we can. Staying up-to-date is one of the best ways to bridge the generation gap.

At any age, it should be our challenge and commitment to climb up that ladder of success not only to develop our potential until the day we die, but to be able to keep up with the fast-paced world we live in as *proactive participants*. You know the old saying, "I'll die with my boots on." Let's add to that, "Climbing the ladder of success."

LESSON #29

INCIDENTALLY,
THERE IS NO TRAINING CLASS

Let's consider two major life events that have no training class. One might be getting married and the other might be having children. You know if each of us had the opportunity to check a crystal ball before either event to see the future, there'd be more than a few of us passing on those two ideas. I remember as a young mother walking my firstborn with a friend of mine walking her firstborn. We were pondering on why we decided to have children. Laughing together, we came to the conclusion it was because everyone else did! I distinctly remember leaving the hospital at age 22 with my first baby and wondering to myself, "Do they have any idea how little I know about this whole baby thing?" Yet, we walk off with little more than motivation and a treasure chest of potential. The only instruction I remember asking before leaving that hospital was how to wash a baby's head to prevent that ugly scaly stuff from forming. Imagine that the uppermost thought in my mind was just keep this baby from growing ugly stuff on her head! Basically the only two pieces of information I was sure about included *what goes in comes out, and it cries.*

Haven't we all learned the hard way? Think about it. I remember having this new baby and being unable to take a shower until about 4 PM. I think back and wonder what on earth I did all day? I guess good knowledge and great experience don't come easily, do they? One thing for sure about this adventurous approach is that we definitely don't unlearn it ever! Great lessons learned!

Marriage is much the same way. Who we are during the *gazing into each other's eyes* stage is one thing. Adapting and changing to life's *new* good and bad habits again requires some learning the hard way and learning through experience. Yet, as we look around, it's easy to see how many people, however amazingly, had such marvelous marriages and child rearing successes. Incidentally, none of those people had training classes did they? Seems unfair but not really. If we really think about how well we hold up under fire and how well we rebound, success can happen for anyone *even if the ducks are not always in a row*. Wouldn't it be convenient if life came with instructions? But it doesn't. Of course, if life did come with instructions, how many of us would toss them out anyhow because we would just assume we could figure it out as we go?

When my daughter worked at Radio Shack during college, she got a close up view of just how mixed up people got themselves when purchasing technology products. She quickly discovered that many of the problems people experienced were associated with the fact that they never read the instructions. Pretty soon she learned the term "RTMs" to describe confused customers. It was inside jargon that meant "read the manual." It is pretty strong evidence that even if instructions are included many of us would just as soon discount them anyway. It's sort of like this love/hate relationship we have with adventure. Sometimes we love that sense of figure it out for ourselves and other times we want to be spoon fed. It's pretty funny when you think about it, isn't it? Many things in our lives we do very successfully without a training class. It certainly proves how capable we are and how successful we can be when faced with the unknown. That pioneering adventure can be tough but many of us do pretty well.

So don't feel too bad for yourself if you feel ill-prepared at times or things get thrown at you that you are bewildered over. Believe in who you are, believe in possibility, pull yourself up by the bootstraps, and get going. Put one foot in front of the other. One of my favorite sayings for life's adventures is, "When the going gets tough, the tough get going." We might not know how and maybe we've never done it or faced it before, but we can achieve tremendous success even if there are *no footprints* in our clean fresh snow. No training class is required if you have winner thinking!

LESSON #30

ARE YOU ADAPTIVE OR MALADAPTIVE?

I remember learning this lesson from my clinical psychologist husband, Steve. I always kid him that I'm *street smart* and he's *trained smart*. However, my husband's insight on two very important clinical words have really helped me when problem solving.

Let me start with a joke I heard many years ago. It was a joke about three POWs who had been taken into the daylight after spending years in solitary confinement. The three were named Bob, Jim, and Joe. So, when they're finally out in the bright sunlight, their captors tell them that there is good news and bad news. The good news is that they get to change their underwear. The bad news is that Bob gets to change with Jim, Jim gets to change with Joe, and Joe gets to change with Bob.

Yep, this is my best example for *MALADAPTIVE*. Action takes place but results don't change much. In fact, the problem often gets compounded when actions are maladaptive and produce more of the same. It makes a great case for monitoring success, doesn't it?

Adaptive, on the other hand, is the planning and execution of ideas and action that bring about *closure* to a given circumstance. Our ability to put something behind us once and for all comes from understanding why something occurs in the first place. By examining our own potential solutions, we can create an outcome that can eliminate the situation from reccurring.

Now whenever I find myself problem solving, I have taught myself to compare my potential solutions from the standpoint of adaptive or maladaptive. I remind myself that the goal is to eliminate a negative and replace it with a positive. Often we just repeat the *smelly underwear* story. We trade one negative for a new negative and create a cycle of negatives rather than a cycle of successes. Then we wonder what went wrong.

Our ability to eliminate bad habits, live healthier, or create new winning habits can be born from our ability to challenge ourselves with adaptive approaches to maladaptive situations or habits. Essentially, we train ourselves to manage the outcome of our lives to successfully bring problems or challenges to positive closure. If perfection doesn't exist because humanity does, then our ability to overcome will ultimately build our success story.

LESSON #31

LOWERING YOUR EXPECTATIONS

You might be thinking from the title of this lesson that this idea just doesn't fit with the notion of winning. At first glance it may appear that lowering expectations has something to do with lowering your standards. However, this lesson has a whole lot more to do with dealing successfully with high standards and perfectionism while operating in the real world with real people and real glitches.

My being married to a psychologist has its benefits. It wasn't so many years ago that we were having a discussion regarding some frustration I was experiencing about some set of circumstances. My husband patiently tossed in the notion that perhaps I should *lower my expectations*. Sometimes the simplest phrase can be so easily misunderstood. My initial reaction was one of, "Are you saying I need to lower my standards?" Interesting how my assumption and translation of this tiny piece of advice was so easily taken incorrectly.

He went on to explain that having high standards is different than lowering expectations, and that the two ideas can co-exist. For example, when we set standards for how we want anything to be done, especially when dealing with others, it's important that we *factor in* the idea that others will never embrace our ideas or standards the same way we do. So if something is very important to us, then we need to take the role of making sure that things proceed the way we intend. Let's not act surprised and shocked then start the blame game.

We then become the person who takes on the responsibility

to make sure the pieces come together as we picture them. Lowering your expectations is about factoring in Murphy's Law rather than being a sitting duck. If anything can go wrong it will and always at the wrong time. Sometimes we make the critical mistake of thinking that because we wanted something badly, planned well, have a fancy title, or are very experienced that we're entitled to just have it work. It's really the opposite. We have to instinctively have an eye for where the *fly in the ointment* will be rather than set ourselves up for disappointment. We have to be willing to monitor, track progress, and follow through. It's so easy to just think it all ought to fall into place. Amazingly, sometimes it does. It would be a mistake to think that everything will always fall into place.

We've got to guard against chewing ourselves up over life's glitches. They're going to happen in the best of circumstances. As we lower our expectations while doing all we can to maintain our dreams and standards, we will then be caught off guard much less and will be better prepared to fix a situation to get ourselves back on track. This lesson will dramatically help cut unnecessary stress and frustration. It will help prevent a negative reflection on ourselves and others.

Nothing works 100% of the time. Those tiny things that don't go as planned are really the small stuff that we need to stop sweating while keeping an eye on the big picture of events. This lesson has really helped me develop my patience and understanding of the reality we face every day. It just doesn't have to rain on your parade.

LESSON #32

MERLIN, MAKE ME A HAWK

Be wise because there is a big picture. Focus is an interesting part of winning. It certainly is easy to get distracted with the everyday garbage we can encounter. Even in this great country of ours, it's so easy to display our own dirty laundry. It's the same thing with our family or workplace. While the big picture can be very good, the underlying imperfections can have us lose focus on the overall picture. There are times when we might have difficulty believing phrases like *this land of opportunity*. I'm not sure I believed that growing up. But it is! We must all guard against the Scrooge and humbug mentality!

I remember when my two children were between the ages of 17 and 23. As a single parent, those years were filled with worry. While I can tell you that I had great kids, at the same time, they were kids. All the applicable discoveries and dangers were there for them, too. I full well realized that my *vote* was counting less and less as they embraced life with a certain careless abandon. So, I worried. But the good news was that while I realized that worry seemed to be part and parcel of those challenging times for our family, I knew that I had to keep focused on the *big picture*. They were great kids and they'd land on their feet. I reminded myself many times that talent, potential, values, ethics, and upbringing would kick in at some point. I had to remind myself of the big picture all the time.

While I could easily have mapped out their little lives on a piece of paper in about 30 minutes, I knew that they could just as easily disagree with me. So, I worried more. I found myself focusing on one very important goal to get through. My goal became to keep the door of communication open no matter what! I'd love to tell you it was easy even though I had good kids, but it wasn't always easy. There was always the balance of what I thought versus what they thought, while allowing them to discover who they were as people. And I know that mistakes are part of discoveries. I also had to come to grips with the idea that they didn't need to be *cookie cutter* kids. I needed to allow enough space for *their wings,* not mine.

Some of life's most challenging issues don't come with a training class. It always saddens me to see families fractured, children disowned, or people using the black sheep label. The big picture is about counting what you have and not about what you don't have or wish you had because someone else does, or you think it ought to be a certain way.

In the play *Camelot*, I love the one scene in which King Arthur is bewildered. As he seeks solitude in the forest, he cries out for Merlin, his teacher, who is no longer around. But as he calls out, he begins to hear Merlin's words in his head. He recalls a time when Merlin would make him a *hawk* flying high over the land. Arthur remembers the beauty he saw from above. Just then he hears Merlin asking him if he sees boundaries or flaws. Arthur remembers answering, "No, Merlin, I just see beauty." At that moment Arthur had made the connection for why Merlin had taught him to fly like a *hawk and see the big picture*. Until then, Arthur thought flying like a hawk was just a delightful fun game to see from way up high.

I love that story. It gives me great consolation and helps recreate the big picture focus rather than *sweating the small stuff, picking at old wounds, or keeping score*. Whether we're in the workplace, a family, a relationship, or a challenge, it's always important to remind ourselves of what the big picture is. We need to count our blessings rather than count our disappointments. So, go ahead, do the hawk exercise whenever you need to see the real beauty below. We've got to take the magnifying glasses off the flaws. We've got to look from afar for proper perspective. I love this lesson and I hope you do, too.

LESSON #33

STOP FOLLOWING THE CROWD

This is an interesting lesson. Seems pretty straightforward. But, in real life application, *herding* comes pretty naturally. It's the no-brainer part of living. Here's what I did, so here's what you do. And while looking around and learning from others is a valuable part of knowledge, the challenge creeps in as to when to duplicate behavior and when not to duplicate what we see.

While facing the challenge of not having the crowd *turn on us* while working to satisfy our need to belong, the real lesson is to fine tune what we observe and make it our own. So many times I've said of myself, "I'm not so smart as I am a quick study. You show me and I can run with it." But, all the while we *run with it*, we need to make it our own. We can make the mistake of taking things too literally, without adding the creative touch to what applies and what doesn't apply for us.

Of course, standing up and being counted come into play here. It's not exactly something we're all comfortable with. Distinguishing yourself and being true to yourself can take thinking and courage. One thing I've learned in business is that *unique sells*. That basically means that you want to stand out in some way from the rest, whether that's in the workplace or in the home, without alienating the masses. Sometimes we follow the crowd because we don't know what else to do or we don't want to rock the boat.

Creativity and innovation are the keys to asking *why* and *how else* before becoming a puppet. I remember one priest commenting to me, before I married at 20, that people where we lived were all *born, brought up, and stayed there.* I remember thinking that he probably meant something I should pay attention to, but I didn't exactly know what it was. It was so easy for me to wonder, "What else is there?" "What else would I do?" or "What's the problem with it anyhow?" Honestly, I had no idea what to do with that piece of wisdom. I recognized it as insightful but had no clue he was describing *herding.* Once again we don't know what we don't know.

I understand very clearly how easy it is for any of us to repeat history. Why? Often it can be because it's the path of least resistance. What we need to learn is that first we should tailor that history, keep the part we like and get rid of the part we don't like, come up with our own plan and commitment, and then make it happen. But sometimes, we live in a world that says *it's good enough, we can get by, or it's not what I want but it'll do.* As I look back, I thank God for the opportunities I was able to capitalize on to customize what I needed to change while maintaining a loyalty and respect for the good from the past.

If what the *crowd* is doing doesn't fit you or your circumstances, then change it! When I was going through a divorce many years ago, it was apparent to me that the *crowd* was fighting like crazy over issues and money. I personally made a commitment that money would not become an issue. Separating dollar for dollar was not what I wanted to do. I wanted freedom of decision making and a smooth transition more than I wanted nickel and diming. There were certainly those cautioning me against such an approach but many years later I know it was right for me. I knew in my heart that my intentions were honest and right for a smoother transition and a softer landing for me and my children.

Learning to think for yourself and maintaining independence

from *the flavor of the day* thinking is probably a great lesson to learn so you can look back and say, "I didn't follow conventional thinking and I'm glad." The defining moments of your life can be born when you don't follow the crowd.

LESSON #34

MISERY LOVES COMPANY

You are who you hang around with. Okay, this may not be new information but the lesson we take from it is that people who become negative or miserable have a way of dragging down those around them. My Dad had a great term for it. He called them *sad sacks*. Sometimes people don't begin as *sad sacks* but they become *sad sacks* over time. They would best be recognized as people who are constantly focusing on problems (created or imagined) and telling their *rotten stories* to anyone anywhere anytime over and over again.

I had a friend many years ago from grammar school through my twenties. Over the years, I came to recognize a pattern developing. Anytime she met a new person, she would roll out her repertoire of *sad sack* stories one after the other. Or, for those of us who were in day-to-day contact, it seemed like every conversation revolved around a doctor appointment, prescription, or potential disease she never had.

I came to realize that this person with whom I'd had lots of fun and laughs through our young adulthood became some-one I could no longer relate to. I had begun my own personal evolution into proactive high achiever thinking and realized over time that we had very little in common. The world she lived in bordered on near misses or past disasters. She went through life looking through the rear view mirror. The world I lived in was about taking action, moving forward, being ex-cited, and building winning relationships. My perspective was about looking ahead.

I have become convinced over the years that if someone can't succeed in a positive way, then they try succeeding any way they can, even if that means being the *best* at having the *worst* disasters.

While winners have their challenges, I've discovered that winners get past their challenges better than most people. One technique I use is to ask myself, "What did I learn?" Once I answer that question to myself, it becomes history and life moves on from there.

The truth is *misery demands company* but it won't get my company. I can think of so many people I know who are truly inspiring, exciting to be around, and offer great conversation. They are like books I get to open and learn something from. They help affirm who I am and offer support in the pursuit of happiness and success. Be good to yourself and affiliate with the best and brightest. I'm betting it'll help you live longer by maintaining positive attitudes and reducing some of life's struggles.

LESSON #35

LOWERING THE HILL

Have you ever thought that something would be so difficult or impossible that you dread even tackling the possibility of it? You've done such a great job of convincing yourself that something is insurmountable that you may even be reducing your own odds of success by not taking advantage of opportunity. I wonder if the idea of failure starts to creep in as the rationale for avoiding certain challenges or opportunities.

I remember, as a little kid, we'd be on a drive somewhere and one thing we did to keep ourselves busy in the car was to look for the big hills coming up. In between the time we located the big hill and the time we finally got to it, it amazingly seemed that the hill didn't look as high any more. As a matter of fact, I remember asking, "Where's that big hill we saw?" Someone would say, "We're on it." I'd say, "How could we be on it, this isn't very high." Only when I turned to look backwards did I see the hill mysteriously reappear, as I realized that we were climbing it. I remember wondering, "How did that big hill get lowered to a small hill?" It was almost anticlimactic.

Thinking back on how my perception changed depending upon where we were in relation to that hill, I've often drawn the parallel that anything from a distance can seem difficult, unknown, or fearful. The truth is that the *closer* we get to understanding something we often realize there is nothing to fear. That holds true for anything scary we face or are unfamiliar with. I remember when my Dad had surgery for colon cancer several years ago. At one point before the cancer was found, a nurse practitioner had recommended to my Dad that he get a colonoscopy. This was about the time a program aired describing colon cancer as, "the disease where people can die from embarrassment." The program showed how people hesitated and avoided getting colonoscopies to prevent and detect colon cancer. My Dad managed to talk his way out of that colonoscopy, only to realize several months later that it probably would have caught his cancer earlier.

Now, the interesting thing about it was the difference in the *hill* or *perception* from a patient perspective or a medical perspective. My Dad imagined this unpleasant and invasive procedure. The truth is the procedure is done with medication that allows complete comfort for the patient. Now that *tiny piece of information* could have made all the difference in helping my Dad deal with *the hill* in his mind. As his children, had we known that, we may have been able to change the outcome, but we didn't know at the time either.

Katie Couric has done a wonderful job *lowering the hill* in this example for all of us. Colonoscopies are becoming more and more common for people over 50. As the word gets out, there seems to be consistency and testimonials that support the view that the procedure itself is a *piece of cake* from a patient perspective. The only real inconvenience is the preparation the day before.

This is a recent example of how we can come to grips with something and realize that our perception was off base. Often, this same perception problem can be the very stumbling block to getting past any of life's dilemmas. We often falsely convince ourselves that there's *no way* we can successfully deal with certain things.

I remember when I began traveling all over the country for my speaking business. I did not see myself as a frequent traveler at all. As a matter of fact, I saw myself quite the opposite. In my own mind, I would try to *endure* travel without grumbling too much. I had one friend who traveled frequently. She was the only person I knew who could offer perspective. So I decided to ask her how she dealt with it. Honestly, I thought surely her answer would match my perspective. I guess I was seeking affirmation of how bad it really was. What I got surprised me. She said, "It's not that bad" in a very convincing tone. I wondered to myself, "Could she be right?"

What I discovered over the next several years, traveling all over the country to hundreds of cities, was that not only was she right, but I had adjusted so well to the routine that I didn't mind it at all. Whenever I told people about my travel, I'd always get the same comments, "I'd hate that" or "How can you stand it?" I see it as one of those *hills* that is just not as high as it may appear from a distance.

When I had surgery for uterine cancer three years ago, I was amazed at how simple the whole thing was. Granted, my cancer was caught very early at Stage 1A (there are 4 Stages). Therefore, I did not require chemotherapy or radiation. While I count myself very fortunate indeed, I still have a certain amount of difficulty having the cancer survivor title. While the fear factor certainly was involved, it was otherwise pretty straightforward surgery and recovery. That *cancer hill* for me was definitely lower than I imagined prior to going through it. I am blown away by the amazing cancer successes these days. The number of people like me, who just walk away with a clean slate because the cancer is caught so early, is higher than I would have imagined. What I did learn was that regular testing is crucial as medical markers for early detection. That was my saving grace.

Fear and the unknown can play some real tricks on us, which makes me conclude that we all have the responsibility to share our awareness, knowledge, and insight with others.

I've learned that winning is easier than it may seem. Personal success can be had by one and all. We can share success by sharing knowledge. It's truly a winning combination. So many challenges or opportunities are much more workable than we may imagine from a distance.

LESSON #36

ARE YOU PIONEERING OR FOLLOWING IN FOOTSTEPS?

We are certainly in fast-paced and challenging times. Sometimes you just want to say, "Enough already." This lesson is about understanding and coping a little better with the times we're up against. We would better be able to deal with difficult times or situations if we simply understood the difference between pioneering and following status quo.

While we'd like instructions or a map to make life as simple as possible, we've got to understand that although we live in a world of convenience, moving at the speed of light, there are times when we won't have instructions simply because instructions don't exist.

One coping skill I use is understanding the difference between *following in footsteps*, which is doing something that's been done before, or *pioneering,* which is doing something that's never been done before. The pioneering is the part that allows us discovery and personal achievement. Now, I didn't say this was easy, but it can become the most rewarding accomplishments we ever enjoy. It's *beating the odds, making it happen, and pushing the envelope.*

If you think about past pioneers, like Columbus discovering America or pioneers discovering the wild, wild West, it's obvious that these are the people pushing the boundaries and challenging the status quo for the benefit of the rest. Certainly, we all enjoy an extra measure of happiness and convenience as a result of their pioneering.

I guess the lesson for the rest of us is about being willing to branch out, take risks to improve things, and generally develop the mentality that sometimes we <u>all</u> have to *push the envelope*. Remember when Rosa Parks *pushed the envelope*? She was an unlikely pioneer, but what she did that day in Alabama changed history. Shannon Faulkner fought for the right to join the all-male Citadel. While she left after a few days, she will always be credited for changing history because she dared to *pioneer* where no woman ever had. While her life was filled for a time with critique and negative press, history has no choice but to count her as a pioneer in our time.

This lesson is about standing and being counted. *Each and every one of us* has the clear responsibility to *pioneer* when faced with the possibility of making this world a better place. Waiting for others can derail the very freedoms and conveniences we all enjoy every day because of those who dared to pioneer before us.

LESSON #37

WHO WRECKED MY MASTERPIECE?

This lesson was indeed a defining moment in my life about 25 years ago. While I was on the fast track as a very successful sales manager and rising star in an international company, I remember very well the turning point that allowed me to catapult myself into the top 1% of sales performers in a field of 12,000 sales managers nationally. While it seemed that my planning was paying off, and pretty much everything I touched was turning to gold, I was beginning to feel satisfied that I had assured my own success into the top ranks. Lo and behold, as I was embracing my new winner thinking and higher standards of sales performance with accompanying financial success, for some unknown reason to me I began experiencing a *slipping factor*. I hadn't changed anything I was doing, so the dilemma I faced was compounded by the fact that it seemed that what once worked beautifully was now in question. Having experienced my first real taste of success at 30 years old, it seemed a real disappointment to me and felt like everything I'd worked for was slipping from my grasp.

While this may seem trivial to some, at 30 years old this felt like something all too close to the word failure to me. I began getting scared. Of course, scared certainly has a way of taking our winner thinking and focus off track by shaking self-confidence to the core. It seemed I agonized for months wondering how to deal with this *something* I couldn't get a handle on.

One Sunday while attending church, and I will never forget this as long as I live, Father Paul Manning told this story.

Once there was a very famous painter who taught students to paint. He was considered a master. Being a student of his was in and of itself defining for those who had the privilege to study under him. One day one of his students created a piece of art that was recognized as a masterpiece. Accolades and recognition abounded. The student was becoming a star. One day when the student arrived to study with the master, he noticed that his masterpiece had been destroyed and was leaning against a wall. Shocked, he approached the master and asked what had happened to his masterpiece. Calmly and patiently the master said, "I destroyed it." Puzzled beyond belief, the young student asked why. The master replied, "Because if I hadn't destroyed it, you'd have thought it was your best."

I walked out of church that day a renewed woman. There was no more agonizing for me. I had come to understand that, yes, masterpieces (like achievements) can be destroyed, but they should never be regarded as our best or final hour. That sermon that day allowed me closure for something I didn't understand and couldn't have prevented. It allowed me to go on. And, I did! Where on earth would I have been without this very powerful lesson that day? I don't know if that priest ever realized the message he delivered that day was a defining moment in my life. It has stuck with me for 25 years and served me very well. I regrouped, changed my focus and direction, and began creating my next masterpiece!

LESSON #38

ARE YOU WAITING FOR
YOUR SHIP TO COME IN?

How many times have we heard this piece of wisdom? I've come to the conclusion that some people actually believe this as if it were a worthwhile lesson. But, there's an important piece missing to this harmless cliché. Can you just picture someone sitting on the dock, day after day, just looking into the horizon for the first glimpse of a ship? I was puzzled because the idea of the quote, I suppose, was to give us hope. But instead it seems kind of depressing and somewhat hope-*less* to be so dependent upon circumstances as to defer our future to the unknown. The good news is that I added on the *real* second half to the saying to make it realistic.

"While you're waiting for your ship to come in, you'd better be sending some out." So there you have it. Finally, something I can live with in the way of discovery, opportunity, and success. Now I've got hope. Now I can use my talent. Now I can attempt to advance the action for myself. Often, success is not a straight shot up but more of a process of elimination as we go. We get to sort through the results we get. We may choose not to pursue some, while we may stumble upon even better results through discovery. This process will help better define which ship you want to come in.

It ties in beautifully with stacking the odds in our favor, rather than limiting our thinking. It's a *multipronged approach* that prevents desperation. If one thing doesn't succeed, then something else might. Whew! I'm glad we cleared that up. We now have a lesson of hope.

When I found myself potentially transitioning from the corporate world to launching my speaking career, I remember realizing that I had to *send the speaking ship* out while I was still in my first career. It occurred to me that I needed to test the waters before deciding to make the change. So just for the heck of it, I launched a speaking career to see if I could make it work. In my mind, I characterized it as dabbling on the side while I was still employed. This *ship I sent out* allowed me to make and view my decision to leave the corporate umbrella behind in a positive way. I created my second career opportunity on *my* terms and in my own way. This was a critical piece in pursuing my new career and transitioning successfully.

These pieces of success all come together from the unlikeliest of places or situations. Every so often when I talk to myself I wonder how on earth I got *here* anyway. *Here* meaning writing this book and having something I feel passionate enough about to share with others. It can feel kind of scary when you send a ship out for the world to see. It can feel pretty daring for someone from Lowell, Massachusetts with no college education, who got her start in business by doing home parties. I still get excited about what ships I can launch next. It's a way of building your ability to let life lead you a little bit.

LESSON #39

GOING FROM
FANTASYLAND TO REALITY

Have you ever heard this one? A dream is a goal without a deadline. I wonder sometimes if we don't just dream to entertain ourselves with pleasant thoughts. Something we wonder and wonder about forever that has absolutely no hope of ever coming true. I suppose I might characterize that as fantasyland. It feels good. It's like our own personal entertainment system. We can play it anytime we want.

We hear people all the time say things like, "I'd love to go to Hawaii," "I gotta get organized," "I gotta quit wasting time," "I gotta get a life," or whatever it happens to be. It's important for all of us to understand that dreams will always remain in fantasyland unless we move them into reality. Sometimes the only thing eluding us is a *plan to succeed,* even if we've never done something before.

So, here are five steps you can use to see where you *get stuck* in the process of success when moving your dreams from fantasyland to reality. As we go through these simple steps, you'll be able to see where your downfall may be. I sincerely believe that once we create awareness of any problem situation, we've taken the first step to solving it.

The first step is asking yourself, "Is it possible?" You're the only one who can answer that.

The second step is to ask yourself, "When?" Often I recommend that people *back into their dreams.* For example, answer this question for me. "If you could have it the way you like it, when would you realistically like to have this happen?" Then you would back into it by breaking your dream into subgoals that you position into place, bearing in mind that adjusting your timetable *is* part of the deal. You see, as you embark on the goal you will then develop a real-time perspective that may alter your original plans. And, that's okay.

The third step is to answer the question "How?" This is the research phase. Here is where you begin digging up all the information you can to help achieve your goal. It could be speaking to others who have succeeded before you, or making phone calls and asking what feels like stupid questions until you gather enough information to start asking some smarter and more informed questions. This step is often a stumbling block because this isn't exactly the fun part. This can feel more like a wild goose chase that poses more questions than answers. Persevering can be a real challenge.

The fourth step is to formulate your plan. Let's say you want to go to Hawaii. You come up with the idea of mowing lawns part-time in the summer to sock away all the money you can for a trip to Hawaii. You decide that it might take you three summers at $1,200 per summer. You further break it down to $400 each of three summer months. That's $100 a week. That's five lawns at $20 per lawn. Now the goal becomes finding five people who will let you mow their lawns weekly for an average of $20 per lawn. Specifics are the key here. Great plan, wouldn't you say? Now, on to step five.

Step five can be the deadliest pitfall of all. As we all know, the best-laid plans do not assure success. All too often, the best-laid plans never get rolled out. We can delay making the first move because we're *too busy.* Yes, great plans can stay on the back burner because we wait for places in our busy schedule to appear magically (like that's gonna happen). So, dreams never get off the ground even with the most talented plan makers, because they never take the two hours to just sit down and get on the phone in *February,* before others get their lawn customers lined up. There's a certain amount of *monomaniac* we have to exert in order to add something else *in.* It's so easy to let life's interruptions thwart our dreams by *not saying "no"* to something at some point in order to create space for the new plan.

Whenever I hear people say their dreams or wishes out loud, the very next questions that come to my mind are, "is it realistic?" and "when?" They are the keys to taking yourself seriously and getting started on the new action plan. Excitement begins when we start to feel that the dream is materializing. That's how I feel right now about this book. It's been ten years of thinking and fantasizing and now six months of writing. The excitement is building as I make this dream of writing a book come true. It's not always easy but, more often than not, it is doable.

So get going, pick that dream out of fantasyland, take yourself seriously, and make it happen. So-o-o-o, have you got a dream in mind? Is it realistic and when?

LESSON #40

PICTURE YOURSELF A WINNER

This technique was presented by a speaker I heard many years ago. I sure wish I could give credit to whomever it was. I guess the point of the message stuck with me, but the name of the person giving it did not. You know it's very interesting how we learn concepts. This speaker's message was about an imaginary camera in your own mind, so you could first *picture yourself* achieving any success you want. It's easy to think everyone knows this, but I don't remember anyone while I was growing up telling me I could be anything I wanted to be.

What it meant to me at the time was that we needed to believe deep inside our gut that success is ours for the taking. This lesson ties in with the concept of becoming a monomaniac to make things happen. *Ho hum* is probably not going do it. *Average bear* doesn't work either. It helps create the focus we need to motivate ourselves to sustain an action that will bring us the desired winning result. This also ties in to having the determination and persistence it takes to believe in something enough to pull it off better than most people would. It's the personal competitiveness that needs to be within us to achieve great things. The greatest competition we'll ever be in is competing with ourselves to pull out our very best. We get to practice every day with every task.

Another part of picturing yourself a winner is to develop the ability to set higher standards for yourself. Higher standards will help distinguish us from the average bear and therefore will help us become leaders of the pack rather than followers. I'm sure many of you can relate to this example. Remember somewhere in your formative years hearing someone in your family reminding you that "even if you shovel garbage, shovel garbage better than anyone ever shoveled garbage." I love it! Often, though, between the time we are exposed to this wisdom and the time of application in our every day existence, we forget the message. Others can be quick to say those functioning at a higher level are just *kissing up,* or question, *"Who exactly do they think they are?"* Another put down is, *"You're making us look bad."*

Peer pressure and guilt are evident everywhere because people forget the wisdom of picturing themselves as winners. It's what we all want and respect, but I wonder if we're really willing to allow ourselves to grab that golden ring, whether it's flipping burgers or anything else we consider unimportant. Every job we have prepares us for the future. Winning breeds winning, and we need to practice it every day to live by this lesson.

You see, the goal is to always give our best. We don't give it to anyone but ourselves, because everything we do well we carry with us toward the next thing we do when giving our best. When we picture ourselves winners, whether we like doing something or not, we develop our potential. We expect ourselves to get very good and be the best. Why? It's because anything less is short-changing us, our families, our communities, our country, and our world. What will you leave in the wake of your life? Will you leave a winning legacy? How will you leave your mark on this world? It's up to you today with every task you do. So you see, the choice is really clear. You deserve to picture yourself a winner. After all, you're sitting on a treasure chest and it's yours! Stretch, grow, and win!

LESSON #41

STOP COMPETING WITH OTHERS
START COMPETING WITH YOURSELF

Have you ever heard this saying, "The grass always looks greener on the other side of the fence." It's interesting that often people repeat a phrase like this over and over again. They don't always apply the wisdom from that saying to their own personal day-to-day success stories. Sometimes, if we focus too much on being number one or beating someone else, we lose focus on the *real win* which is *beating our best,* whatever that *best* happens to be. Over the last 35 years I've noticed how common it is for people to spend too much time watching what other people are doing and wondering why they don't have what others have. Recognizing the breaks others get more than recognizing your own breaks can develop into an unhealthy envy of others' success, and corrupt your own ability to better your best with what you're facing.

A cliché that more aptly fits reality is the "bloom where you're planted" thinking. This certainly allows for looking around our environment and learning from others. The key is to take that information and make it yours. Will your success match theirs? Maybe it will and maybe it won't.

I can remember one business situation I was in for several years in which several of us shared a specific sales territory. While I was in the number one position in volume sales, the others began criticizing my approach. Their interpretation of my lead was that I was doing something that wasn't right. The truth was that my approach was different from theirs. My tendency was to try new things. My basic belief was that bad ideas had no problem dying on their own. Even the best ideas could be a challenge to get up and running. What was amusing to me was how much focus was placed on my success, rather than figuring out how they could succeed at the same or higher level.

I've always believed that there's plenty of business to be had. Too many people settle for status quo, check some rulebook, or wait for others to give them permission to proceed. I can remember very well seeing new business ideas come down from above that opposed previous thinking but all of a sudden it became the thing to do. So many times I thought to myself, "I've thought of that before" but never tried it because I was not taking the risks I needed to progress. These were real turning points for me. I realized that the only person I was competing with was myself.

An interview on television recently featured one of the Olympic athletes saying how he learned to compete with himself as part of his personal success story. I thought to myself, "*Amen.*" Let's stop trying to copy what others have, or unconsciously develop envy that simply derails our focus off the real goal of beating our best. You can never be disappointed when you are true to yourself, your own discovery, and your own approach, while simultaneously learning from others. We can borrow from the best or the worst. We just need to know how to implement it within the scope of our own goals.

It's so easy to look around and see what others have and think *we* should have it. You can have what others have, but getting it may take a different road than their road. For example, a son steps into a successful family business. Wouldn't we all love to have something handed to us? Well, if that doesn't happen, then we've got to open our own doors. We can achieve the goal of owning a successful business, and maybe then our children can step into a successful family business. Maybe if *you* can't have it, then you can make it happen for your children. Here comes that *pioneering* again. It's the painful task of putting one foot in front of the other when we wish it would be easier. While it's very human to wish for easier, I've figured out that when I learn something the hard way, I never forget it. We have all learned the hard way, but the key is to become a victor anyway.

The world provides us with a *menu*. Choose what you like and don't like. Buckle down and start competing with yourself to achieve whatever is important to you. The good news is you don't have to be so smart, as you have to be a quick study *and* figure out how to incorporate what you learn from others into your own masterpiece. Hats off to the those who have already implemented this great lesson.

LESSON #42

STRAIGHTENING PRIORITIES
WITH MARBLES

This is a wonderful story I heard awhile ago that is worth repeating. It's the story about a man who had a jar of marbles to represent the remaining weekends left in his life. He figured out the number of years he could live and multiplied it by the number of weekends in a year. He then put one marble in the jar for each remaining weekend. Every weekend after that he would remove one marble. It created a sense of focus and priority for doing things he wanted to do, not just doing things he had to do. It created an emphasis on smelling the roses and enjoying life, because the marbles will eventually run out.

You know, like many things we hear and forget, this one stuck with me. If you take a simple figure of 80 years of life and break it down into four quarters (20 years each), then I'm in the third quarter. I must admit I have become painfully aware of taking advantage of opportunity to do what I enjoy.

Flowers are something I now enjoy that a fast-paced corporate life never allowed. Reading 10 books in a row to my grandchildren would be difficult were it not for my very flexible speaking career. Going to friends' and relatives' weddings all over the country has more meaning. Going to family reunions or calling friends also has more meaning. Now is the time because the marbles are going fast. Shoulda and coulda don't apply here.

So what will you do this weekend to make your marble count? Make a difference in someone's life and you'll make a difference in your own. Get off that computer and talk to people face to face. Laugh, touch, feel, cry, enjoy, and most importantly, live to not regret anything.

LESSON #43

ISN'T IT ALL JUST COMMON SENSE?

Ever ask yourself this question? Common sense seems so obvious to those of us who have it. This is probably one of the main critiques I hear from managers when discussing training for employees.

Now, I'm not sure if this is the good news or the bad news, but I've come to the conclusion that the answer is simple. The answer is, "No, it's only common sense if you've heard it before." There are so many life lessons to learn. There are so many experiences to be had that educate us and build us as people. What seems so obvious to one seems to elude the other.

We've got two choices: coach the person the best way we can or accept the status quo. Life is a choice. However, I believe we can bring people up to an improved level of performance. It may not be as high a level of common sense as someone else's, but we can certainly build awareness and improve the level of functioning. We have to care enough to find what works for that person. We have to be skilled at teaching.

By the way, did I mention that teaching is not easy to do? I recently tried to teach my grandson how to tie his shoelace. What an eye-opener that was for me. Being on autopilot doing something like that and trying to translate it into simplistic terms is definitely not easy. Another example is my youngest grandson trying to put on his own velcro-tie shoes. He has asked me a million times, before putting them on, whether or not he's got them lined up correctly. Again, a very important reminder that this stuff is not easy, even for a kid who *wants to get it right*. He doesn't want to wear his shoes on the wrong feet and it is difficult to train his eye to catch the difference.

When presenting to audiences, I very much realize that awareness, knowledge, application, and repetition go hand-in-hand with influencing others to do anything.

My brother was a born carpenter. Don't know where he got it. He just has it. Whenever I watch him work, I can't help but be amazed at how easy he makes it look, because building to me seems complicated. Now, while I would never be the carpenter he is, it's pretty obvious that if I worked with him 40 hours a week for 5 years, I'd certainly improve my ability to build things.

Therein lies the key lesson. There is no substitute for repetition and time in as keys to skill building. Helping someone develop new and better habits takes patience and skill. Part of the challenge comes from trying to understand where they're coming from and finding out exactly what missing links they need to succeed. It can be quite a long way from introducing information to having it become common sense. All of us are smart about certain things and not so smart about other things. Some things come to us easily and some things just don't.

LESSON #44

THE LOTTERY MENTALITY

I suppose the state lottery that has been around for quite some time now has demonstrated the power of *a dollar and a dream*. As we look around us, it's evident how many people dream of that big win. One ticket is all you need, I guess, even though the odds are one in seven gazillion million.

As I continue to develop in my own take-charge, high-achiever mentality, I chuckle at the idea that people hold on to a ticket they paid a dollar for and actually believe this could be it. Talk about the odds being stacked against you! And, we pay money for those incredibly ridiculous odds.

Truth is, we probably have a better chance of being struck by lightning or becoming the ruler of a small country. I remember times when my husband bought lottery tickets and as the 11 PM news would come on, he'd ask me to watch for the numbers. Frankly, I don't know how I kept myself from laughing hysterically. I mean, if you really consider how ridiculous the whole notion of being picked is, it'd be difficult to muster the energy to participate to begin with. Of course the winners who are put on display look like you and me, and naturally, they're believers. But just like in sales, there's that interesting little habit of showcasing the *incredible feat* as a day-to-day example of a norm that is not reality.

Anyway, am I telling people not to play the lottery? It may sound as if that's what I'm doing, but it's not. What I am trying to get across in this lesson is that if we can actually have *hope in our hands* holding a lottery ticket, then imagine the odds we can stack in our favor every single day of the week if we use the personal power we possess to stack the odds *in our favor*. Now, believe me, if my husband ever won a lottery, I'd never refuse the money. However, we can certainly use our potential and power every day to advance the action in our lives and inch our way to something better. The lottery mentality can actually harm us if we're not taking day-to-day action to improve our existence.

I think we need to be careful of that *ship coming in* thinking. It can disable us as we wait for the big one to come to us, instead of creating lots of little day-to-day successes that really can have tremendous impact on our lives now. We need to believe in ourselves as winners with or without a lottery ticket in our hands.

Yes, as you probably guessed, I don't buy lottery tickets. Buying lottery tickets makes me feel hopeless and dependent on outside events when I can be taking proactive action. It's certainly worth considering that our real hope lies in the power of our own hands. I hope this lesson helps you *see your own hands* as being more powerful than any lottery.

LESSON #45

GO AS FAR AS YOU CAN SEE,
THEN YOU'LL SEE HOW FAR YOU CAN GO

Not only do I have fond memories of this lesson, but also of the person who drove it home in the kindest way. Throughout the climb in my sales career no one was more shocked than I was at the successes I pulled off. At the same time, I clearly remember tremendous apprehension learning to better my best. I was constantly bogged down with thoughts of being too greedy or too pushy, because I already felt I had achieved at levels far beyond anything I could imagine.

Fear was a regular visitor whenever I considered a higher goal. At times, other people believed in me more than I ever believed in myself. The good news is that has changed over the years. My husband has now taken over the role of believing in me more than I do sometimes.

I had the great fortune to know a wonderful man, named Joe Hara, who was the International President for Tupperware Home Parties during the '80s. Joe always provided such a calming effect for reaching higher. He would stand on stage before thousands of people and would support our efforts by repeating year after year, "Go as far as you can *see,* then you'll *see* how far you can go."

What I got from Joe was learning to trust myself to figure it out as I went along. Rather than being gripped by fear or becoming complacent, I was able to carefully nudge myself to the next level. Joe taught us to set goals and trust in our ability to figure it out. So many times in the last 15 years I have thought of his inspiration. It still allows me to keep believing in my own dreams.

Picture yourself standing and looking at Niagara Falls. What you see is water falling in two different places and you wonder where all this water comes from. Now picture yourself climbing an observation tower at Niagara Falls where you can see the Niagara River split around Goat Island to create the American Falls on one side and Canadian Falls on the other side. Without climbing that observation tower, it's a real mystery as to where all that water comes from.

Setting goals and reaching new heights always expands our knowledge and understanding. They are very exciting indeed. They keep us young and fresh and believing in possibility every day we live. Joe Hara is one of my heroes. What wonderful lessons he taught. I still get a kick out of the prospect of climbing that *next* flagpole to see how far I can see. Oh, and thanks for the memories.

So, go as far as you can see, then climb the flagpole to see what's in the distance. You'll figure it out as you go because you're a winner!

LESSON #46

WHEN YOU'RE GREEN YOU'RE GROWIN'

When you're green you're growin', when you're not you rot. Thank you, Dianna Calle, because I love this one. It may seem that growing depends on being in the right place at the right time, but it's really more about uncovering opportunity. It's developing our ability for expansion. It's being clever and innovative by advancing the action despite obstacles.

It's turning every stone to test the waters and make discovery. It's being curious enough to *see what happens if* and *how else* you can make something happen. Too many times people settle too soon, don't rock the boat, and take too literally the thinking of the day. And while I think it's important to respect and take stock of the knowledge and experience of others, we must learn to challenge the status quo if we think the possibility exists. After all, discoveries are made every day by people like you and me.

It's our right to question what we hear, validate experience with others, and educate ourselves sufficiently to start asking smart questions. It's not uncommon, for example, to take a doctor's word as law. More and more people are taking a proactive role in their own health care by asking what other options they have. One story I knew of was about a woman in New York whose family doctor confirmed breast cancer and recommended a radical mastectomy. After being encouraged to get a second opinion at Roswell Cancer Institute in Buffalo, the woman discovered to her delight that a radical mastectomy was not necessary and that a lumpectomy was an option. Without the presence of mind to validate information and question the first recommendation, this woman would have been scarred unnecessarily. Another person I knew was told by her doctor that she had six months to live due to Stage 3 breast cancer. It was friends in Florida who recommended a specialist at the Moffitt H. Lee Cancer Center & Research Institute near Tampa. It was that specialist who offered the first glimmer of hope for this woman in her 50s. He recommended surgery, chemotherapy, radiation, and a bone marrow transplant. That was five years ago — and she continues to do well and live a normal life. Both these cases had vastly better outcomes as a result of uncovering opportunities.

Most of us can learn this habit day-to-day by thinking for ourselves while asking questions. It doesn't require that we become defiant or rude. We just need to be logical, listen to our own gut, network with others, and dig for information as we spread the word nationwide.

I've discovered in the workplace that people often guess when responding to a question. Our only mistake is completely accepting what we are told and not double checking or questioning it for accuracy. We should *proof the spoken word* and test the waters to see what'll fly. There are often options relevant to any issue if we simply speak up to make our needs known. I just discovered in changing insurance companies that insurance brokers do things quite differently. As I was getting frustrated with the initial information I got, I discovered there were other agencies more compatible with my needs. It's only in the diehard pursuit that we discover and get what we're really looking for.

Where I grew up, I don't remember one person telling me about possibilities, options, and financing for college. That was a world I knew nothing about. What's difficult about that reality is that the knowledge existed then. It just didn't exist in my world. Growth and development were stifled for many of us. This could account, in part, for why people just accept what is apparent without digging and discovering. Opportunities are everywhere. Lucky for me one day that I was in the right place at the right time. It's really kind of scary to me when this is the way we get a break, that is, someone virtually rescuing us. When I was about 17, I worked for an attorney for about six months and I regularly did errands at the Post Office on business. One day while at the Post Office, the person taking care of me said, "What are you doing making peanuts there? Why don't you take your civil service test and get a higher paying job?" I will never forget that person's face as long as I live. While I didn't know him and he didn't know me, he cared enough to offer valuable advice to someone he saw as deserving more. It took quite a bit of courage for him to say what he did. Sure enough, I took my civil service test and scored high enough that I didn't have to wait to be called from a list. Within a few months, my life and job had changed for the better. Thanks to that stranger in the Post Office, I was green and growin'.

I discovered that being talented in and of itself is never enough without lots of opportunity. As in this case, opportunity came from a very unlikely place. Fortunately for me, I was a quick study and took advantage of that person's advice that day. I wish I could thank him for what he awakened in me. He cared enough to help a kid who didn't know better.

Once you discover the feeling of making things happen, it can be a real adrenalin rush. Beating the odds is something we all have to learn. Being an opportunist involves becoming determined, persistent, knowledgeable, and methodical all rolled into one. It's *being on the lookout* for opportunities to advance in the Game of Life. It's our ability to learn new things along with the younger generation, taking advantage of e-mail at any age, learning computers, and staying young. When I see the elderly working with computers, I say "YES!" You all are my heroes. It's so easy to say, "Oh, I don't bother with that at my age." Nonsense! Seize the moment, find the opportunity, and learn something new. It's a great way to live when you're green and growin'!

LESSON #47

WHO EVER TOLD YOU IT'D BE EASY?

No one! How simple is that? Well, that's what I tell myself when I start to get overwhelmed about something. It helps me regroup, go back to the drawing board, and get logical rather than emotional.

What we have difficulty with sometimes is that we just forget that some things will be difficult, no matter how talented we are or how many titles or accolades we have. The funny thing is sometimes we're taken down by something simple or something obvious that we just miss and we actually get angry with ourselves, as if we're supposed to be perfect.

I feel like life tests us all the time. No kidding. I remember telling my children while they were growing up that challenges helped build strength of character. Of course, hearing that enough times made them want to throw up. I'm hoping this tip became more meaningful to them as they faced more challenges. Everyone needs to be reminded of this from time to time. We can easily lose sight of it.

Being blindsided by life's challenges never seems to be opportune and it's easy to get caught off guard. It becomes easier to fall into the victim mentality of "Why me? It isn't fair." Positive self-talk at this point becomes a critical survival skill to help get through any challenge whether it relates to health, work, relationships, education, personal, or the unknown.

The goal is always to be better and stronger because of a challenge, rather than be taken down by it. I remember a segment on one of the television news magazines that did a story about a young woman who was married, had children, and had been born with no arms. The segment showed how functional she had become. She was a mother who took care of her child, drove, and did just about everything you and I do. She learned to use her feet like we use our arms. It was an amazing and incredibly enlightening story. It sure proved to me how those of us with every opportunity probably limit ourselves without ever realizing it. That story pointed out to me that *the sky's the limit.* We can push ourselves to achieve remarkable accomplishments against the odds and in the face of the unknown.

Inspiration is everywhere every day. People everywhere accomplish remarkable things. The interesting piece is that people make it look easy while the rest of us can't even imagine. So, while things may not always be easy we must accept the fact that unfortunate things happen to good people all the time. Have faith in the doable, and be inspired by success around us. While no one ever said it would be easy, always remember you're sitting on a treasure chest of potential and discovery. Thinking and believing in possibility will always help you advance the action in the direction of a win!

LESSON #48

TAKE CHARGE
TO CREATE YOUR OWN LUCK

A recent personal example of putting my *take charge* strategy into action were the events surrounding 9/11. The beginning of September, 2001, happened to be a full schedule for me that included 12 flights from September 10 to September 19. Murphy's Law was definitely up and running for me during that time. My first flight was on September 10 from Newark, New Jersey (where one plane was hijacked) to Seattle, Washington for a program.

The morning of September 11, I was back at the Seattle Airport at 6:30 AM Pacific time (9:30 AM Eastern time) for a Southwest flight to Spokane, Washington for a program at 12:30 PM. Just prior to boarding, it was announced that the airport was being shut down and it was unclear as to when it would reopen. Information was sketchy at best. Realizing that I had to get to Spokane soon, I approached a few passengers in line to see if anyone was driving to Spokane, about five hours away. Luckily for me, two salesmen in line had appointments in that area and one had a car at the airport. They agreed to take me along with them. Another young lady in line heard me approach them and she also asked if she could ride along because she lived in Spokane and was going home. So, off the four of us went in a car at about 7:30 AM Pacific time (10:30 AM Eastern time). Two of us in the car had cell phones, so it was only during the drive to Spokane that information about the seriousness of the attacks began to reach us. The first call I got was from my daughter who, after speaking to my son, was frantic to reach me. They knew I was flying to the west coast but didn't remember if it was on

9/10 or on 9/11. I realized hearing her voice that this was the first time in my children's lives that world events seriously impacted and rocked their world. Then, over the course of the next few hours, what had really happened began sinking in. I realized immediately when I heard that planes flew into the World Trade Center that no American pilot would ever fly a plane into those buildings. Living outside Buffalo, New York and having worked in New York City many times, I immediately realized that 20,000 to 30,000 people were in those towers. Like every American, I was more horrified as news unfolded.

Still unsure of what to do stranded so far from home, I felt at least some security arriving at my destination in Spokane by 12:45 PM to present my program to a waiting audience. I was somewhat shell shocked, but people were very concerned and caring. My next challenge was getting back to Tacoma for two more programs the next day. My contact in Spokane offered to drive me half way at 10 PM after my program, and I was swapped off at about 12:30 AM with my contact for the next day. I arrived back in Tacoma, Washington by 2:30 AM to present on Wednesday morning at 10 AM, 9/12. Word seemed to indicate that airports would reopen on Thursday and I felt hopeful about my return flight to Buffalo. So, after completing my last program at about 10:30 PM that evening, I called Continental Airlines to confirm my flight from Seattle on Thursday, 9/13. I was on hold for 35 minutes before getting the news that the first flight they could offer me was on the following Tuesday, 9/18. Now I realized just how bad off I really was. I was stranded, I had very little clothing, and would have to live in Seattle for 6 more days! It also meant I would miss the following week's three engagements in Texas. Next, I called Amtrak and was on hold for 40 minutes to discover that getting a train offered no better hope. My final option was renting a car and driving home. I called Hertz at midnight to inquire what it would cost to rent a car from Tacoma to Buffalo. I was quoted about $600. Even that seemed reasonable, because living in Seattle had a price and I had little clothing. When I asked about how many miles away Buffalo was and I was told about 2,500 miles, I lost it. I was laughing so hard I was crying at how ridiculous this whole predicament was. I could barely recompose myself to continue the reservation. I had absolutely no clue if I could drive 2,500 miles alone Thursday morning and get home by Sunday to be able to fly out on Monday morning 9/17 for my programs in Texas. It was the best shot I had and I was just angry enough to do whatever I could to cut my losses. I felt so stranded that I just wanted to get home.

So, yes, Thursday morning at 7:30 AM, I picked up my rental car (and they were going fast) and drove home alone to Buffalo. The first day I made it about 650 miles to Bozeman, Montana. The second day I made it about 900 miles to Sioux Falls, South Dakota. The third day I made it 900 miles to my son's in Cleveland, Ohio. The fourth day I drove the final 230 miles, and I arrived home Sunday morning at 10:30 AM, having driven 2,680 miles in 3 1/2 days. I caught up on some work, slept in my own bed, and then got to the airport at 4:30 AM Monday morning to fly to Texas. It was my first flight after 9/11 and I was scared to fly. The pilot of that Air Tran flight thanked us profusely for showing up. I thought to myself, "If you can show up, then I can show up." Those terrorists had no right shutting down our country or our economy. I couldn't prevent 9/11 but I could reduce the negative outcomes to our economy by living my life.

Pick yourself up by the bootstraps and take charge rather than settling for less or focusing on what you can't control. You'll develop your winner thinking for becoming a *victor over circumstances* rather than a *victim of circumstances*.

LESSON #49

INGREDIENTS FOR CREATING YOUR OWN LUCK

While perfection doesn't exist and people don't always get what they shoot for even with the best thought out plans, we must always believe in possibilities. We've got to be curious enough to wonder why something didn't work out, be willing to test a few alternatives to see if we get the same result, proof the information received for accuracy, be willing to take risks, and be determined to keep trying.

Setback is a word we understand pretty clearly. When setbacks occur, it's a little harder to talk ourselves into hot pursuit. More often than not, with enough resistance from those around us, we start telling ourselves, "If it's not meant to be then it's not meant to be."

Abraham Lincoln's life is a stunning example of achieving success after many setbacks. The personal tragedies and lost elections during his life before being elected the 16th President of the United States are almost unbelievable. History holds him in very high regard. He *created his own success*. No one handed it to Abraham Lincoln. Having to create our own luck is much more common than we may think. I'm not sure we even realize just how common it is for people to have to make it completely on their own, with nothing handed to them. It's so easy to think otherwise and feel bad for ourselves.

Years ago I remember reading the story of Joan Rivers' life as she was beginning her career as a stand-up comedian. There were times when she had no money, no food, and was staying in dumpy hotels. Now, this is not about whether or not you like Joan Rivers. What she went through to create her own success was tough stuff. She made an incredible set of circumstances finally pay off. We need to learn about people's successes and what they went through to help inspire us to believe in our dreams and be curious enough to wonder how we can pull them off.

Here's an example of how creating your own luck might apply day-to-day. I remember one time while my son was in high school he wanted to have his car painted. So, I recommended he check around for prices to consider whether or not the possibility was worth it based on the car's value. I personally had no idea what having a car painted would cost. But I do remember him coming home after checking it out and feeling dejected at the price he was quoted. He could see his great idea going up in smoke, based on that quote. He was very disappointed. I knew this was important to him. So, I taught him the lesson of perseverance if he wanted this so much. I suggested that he get several estimates and go to smaller shops. I recommended that he let them know he wanted to do this as inexpensively as possible to spruce up the car. It was really his first lesson in how estimates can vary *so* much. Frankly, I find myself shocked rather frequently when getting estimates. It's incredible how much they can vary for the same thing. Sometimes we forget there can be such a wide range when pricing something. Sure enough, he was able to find someone to do the job at a very reasonable price. He was very happy and learned a very important lesson about what it took to create his own luck and reach his goal.

This is a very big world we live in. *Pull-yourself-up-by-the-bootstraps* success is everywhere and much more common than we might believe. I think it's way too easy to think *the rich get richer,* which can cause us to abdicate responsibility for even trying. The ingredients for creating your own luck, opportunity, advancement, improvement, or ultimate success are right in your treasure chest of potential. This lesson teaches that luck can spin off of setbacks, rejection, and lack of support or opportunity.

Now that we understand *luck* and put it in a clearer light, get gutsy. No pain, no gain! No guts, no glory! Go ahead and *dig in* to create your own luck each and every day for personal and professional success. One thing is for sure, it's probably *not* going to arrive Special Delivery on your doorstep.

LESSON #50

DOES FEAR RULE YOU?

When we fear something, we accept the way it is, we accept status quo, we avoid it, and we choose not to change it. We signal approval and acceptance by allowing something to continue on the same path. You hear people all the time saying, "Oh, that always happens," as if we're settling because there's no improvement in sight. Passivity is at the heart of letting fear take over. We tell ourselves it won't matter anyway, we don't care that much, we don't want to rock the boat, and we squash our own needs, thoughts, value, self-image, and rights.

Of course, there will always be times when passivity is okay. If someone asks where we should eat, one response might be "It doesn't matter." But even with that, we should be careful of always saying, "It doesn't matter." Never having an idea or opinion breeds a passivity that says, "I don't count." People who always go along don't always realize the *paralysis* that occurs from fear of speaking up, taking a stand, influencing others, and getting more of what they want or need. The key, though, is that once we decide to speak up or get fear out of the way, we need to approach it in a diplomatic and caring way. I can think of people who never speak up, then all of a sudden, out of nowhere comes some wise remark that could stop traffic. Everyone wonders where on earth it came from. I wonder if it isn't about allowing ourselves to get *fed up* rather than being understood as we go.

Fear of speaking up or taking a stand can result in a real lack of honesty with others. Can you think of that couple married 35 years where the wife never spoke up and they never had an argument? Lo and behold, once the kids are gone, so is she. All of a sudden the "you never cared about me" comes flying out. Once again, where on earth does that come from?

Of course there are those who lack any fear at all and probably suffer from foot-in-mouth disease. So, we're talking about a fine line here as we distinguish the assertive approach to take to participate in this world of ours. It's interesting that you will hear people comment, "You know he might be rough around the edges, but at least you know where you stand." It is testimony that people prefer honesty to lack of honesty.

Why does fear rule our choices? Perhaps we don't realize that we're putting the preferences of others above our own. While we all certainly cater to others for lots of reasons, we must carefully analyze our method of operation. If we defer to others all the time, then we become people who can easily be taken advantage of by those who speak up for what they want or prefer. The victim mentality can overtake us and sometimes have us believe we truly are helpless against the world. It can result in us believing that what we want doesn't matter and what we try to change won't change anyway. Essentially, we allow fear to rule our ability to function and be counted among those who make a difference.

Now am I telling you that speaking up is easy? No, because the more introverted we are by nature, the more it feels like we're out there naked for the world to see. It can feel awkward and we don't like it, so we avoid it. The truth is the backlash is probably worse than coping with that fear in a healthy way.

This lesson is really about knowing (1) when to let go without developing a pattern of passivity, and (2) that we can't let fear keep us from being *counted* on this planet. We must value ourselves and our ideas before others will ever value us. So, if you decide to kick fear out of your way once and for all, remember, the best of all worlds is removing fear *before* we get fed up with what's going on and lash out or explode. To replace needless fear, we need to give ourselves the respect, value, caring, and diplomacy that come from a healthy ego.

LESSON #51

ARE YOU IN SLOW REVERSE?

If you're not moving forward, then you're probably in reverse. Only problem is sometimes we're moving in reverse so slowly that we can convince ourselves that we're *holding our ground.* Here's where the lesson comes in. Embracing change and progress as we commit to personal and professional excellence is about moving forward. We spend our time getting excited about possibility and small changes that ultimately add up to a lifetime of successes and lessons for others.

Moving forward, then, is how the proactive high achiever operates on a daily basis. It's so easy to say to ourselves, "I'd rather be a couch potato." It's as if sitting and relaxing too much on the *road to progress* don't create a bigger chance for getting run over by those who pass us by.

Anything worth having is going to take real commitment and effort. We often wait for someone or something to *part the seas* before we begin so that everything is easy and simple. The human side tells us to *take it easy and don't kill yourself.* The achiever within is going to make things happen rather than settle for less.

Sometimes we might settle for less. We just need to be mindful of how frequently we take the easy way out when avoiding achievement because we think it's going to be too hard. I wouldn't be writing this book if I caved in to the "but how long is it going to take?" whine. At the same time, putting off writing this book would keep me from reaching the next level.

These days many examples of the *slow reverse process* come to mind. People who don't have computers, aren't skilled in keyboarding, don't use e-mail, or can't operate a VCR are already among those on the outside looking in. These are people for whom doors are closing. It's so easy to convince ourselves that it's only a couple of things when it's really about *not boarding the ark* as the flood waters of progress rise. The next step in slow reverse is starting to feel we're too far behind to catch up, so then we begin to qualify something as a lost cause or *not worth it anymore.*

Certainly, I can relate to the challenge with the technology boom. It was only about 15 years ago, while managing a staff and distribution business, that I was making statements like, "Oh, I don't even turn the computer on because I have Cookie (my computer operator) and she's great." It wasn't too long after that when I started realizing that in the speaking business it's important to have a working knowledge of what people face day-to-day with technology. Keeping up and being knowledgeable are critical for staying ahead.

I often wondered growing up at what age someone started getting old. I've come to the conclusion that it is whenever we allow ourselves to be left behind the times. Now that I've defined that in my head I feel like I've discovered the fountain of youth. If *you're as young as you feel*, then you must continue your quest to discover and grow as long as you live and breathe on this earth.

So now I've discovered the benefit to me in the long run. I'll be happier pursuing achievement and it'll keep me young longer. Bingo! Slow reverse is like taking *our spunk* and tucking it back into our treasure chest for a rainy day. I've also found that the people who are not excited and moving forward are the same people who live to make up excuses on

how the world is *chewing them up and spitting them out.*
They begin looking back upon the *good old days* as the time
when they were comfortable. However, this is a huge red
flag that people are losing their ability to relate in the present.
Alot of years of slow reverse will definitely bring us to this
juncture.

As we look our loved ones in the eyes, it is imperative that
each and every one of us works very hard to make this world
a better place than we got it. It's not just up to everybody
else. Slow reverse is settling for less and passing it on. It's
like hand-me-downs or leftovers.

Feel good about who you are and what you can accomplish.
Be excited to live in a country in which opportunity is everywhere. All we have to do is show up and put our best foot
forward to secure a better world for those who come after us.

Think about the generation that fought World War II, and all
the heroes from conflicts before and after World War II, who
made this country of ours what it is. We owe them our very
best. The good news is that for most of us no one is shooting
at us. Instead, it's just another computer glitch to figure out!

LESSON #52

DO YOU WANT IT BADLY ENOUGH?

As I think back over the thousands of sales people I had the privilege of working with during my career, I remember meeting so many capable and talented people. I found a few main reasons why some people achieved success and why success eluded so many others. So here we go. In both my observations and reflections of my own success, a few things became evident to me.

First, people often do not believe in their own ability. Often our own ability is recognized first by other people not personally connected to us. They seem to identify something we haven't yet identified in ourselves. So we tend to put up our guard rather than take their comments seriously. We might choose to believe there is a hidden agenda. We might choose to believe they don't know what they're talking about. We might be suspicious that they're up to something we haven't yet figured out. We can easily discount their insight. It's easier that way.

Second, if it's pioneering, we're sort of half in and half out at the same time. Our commitment becomes *a wait-and-see* approach. We wait and see if the *stars line up* or something. In other words, we don't really stick to something long enough to fairly assess the possibilities and problem solve issues. We really don't allow ourselves a fair assessment of the ups and downs. We really don't want it badly enough to figure it out. I always told people that if they could give something up on their best day, then it would be a decision based on logic rather than emotion. If, however, we want to cave in because we're frustrated, discouraged, or stressed, then it's more of a decision based on emotion rather than logic.

Third, peer pressure can be a real deterrent. When I started my speaking career, there were only a few who recognized the compatibility between my style and my speaking choice. I can count on one hand the number of people who encouraged me. As a matter of fact, for a long time most people never asked how I was doing or showed much interest in how I was opening this speaking door. Of course I realize it's a pretty non-traditional career. When people think of speakers they may think of Zig Ziglar. Now, remember they think of Zig Ziglar after he became known, had credibility, and had written books. Somehow, it's hard to match those credentials with your neighbor. It took a lot of determination to go it alone and continue to believe in myself. What helped was telling myself that the only difference between the Zig Ziglars of the world and me was *time in* and *paying my dues.* If others don't take our dreams seriously, it can be more difficult for us to hang on to them.

Fourth, if you grew up feeling like you were not smart enough or good enough, it can be extremely difficult to overcome or shake that feeling. Perhaps we exercise too much caution before we venture too far from what we know or what we're used to. Perhaps we can't envision success with our name attached to it. Unconsciously the known will always be more comfortable than the unknown. So, we stick with the known, whether we agree with it or not, because it's easier.

Know what you dream of doing, having, or being. Be honest, sincere, and genuine about your own intentions. Put the negatives in perspective. Believe in yourself. Develop your sense of adventure and discovery. Want it so badly that you can taste it. Develop the ability to be determined and persistent in your pursuit. I remember once having it explained as becoming a monomaniac about a goal. I've come to understand that a great deal more over the last few years. You've got to feel it in your gut and not be deterred by obstacles. It's how wars are won. It's how we succeed at just about anything.

LESSON #53

THE ART OF PICKING BRAINS

Hey, this looks easy. I'll pick Albert Einstein's. Or, I could pick Bill Gates'. Well, that's not really what this lesson is about. Although given the opportunity, I sure would love to *pick their brains* for ideas, mindset, tips, and techniques relevant to how they did what they did.

The art of *picking brains* is more about being willing to network and talk to people who've been there and done that. My first reaction to this idea was, "Why would they want to tell me anything?" "Why should they care enough to help me?" "They'll think I'm stupid." What I've discovered over the years is that people most often are flattered that anyone even cares enough to ask. I occasionally get asked how I became a professional speaker. I'm always happy to tell people about my experiences as a way of shedding light on their question. I can certainly think of many people who have been very open with me over the years by sharing their insights.

I remember very early in my speaking career when Dr. Terry Paulson was speaking at a local program I attended. He seemed *light years ahead* of me. At the time I knew no other big name speakers, so I decided to ask him at the break if he needed a ride back to the airport, which I did, because I wanted to *pick his brain*. He had never met me in his life. Frankly, I felt like I was asking a stranger on a date! To my absolute shock, he said yes. We chatted a short time before I dropped him off at the airport. Terry Paulson may have thought I was crazy that day, but I was eternally grateful for his insight and wisdom. He helped me push a door open that felt incredibly hard to open.

Another speaker who I had the privilege to meet was Al Walker. Coincidentally, both Terry and Al were members of the National Speakers Association. I met Al at a small gathering locally and, as we walked out of the hotel together, I told him my dream of becoming a speaker. He said, "You've got it, you'll do it." Man, that was as close to God coming down to put an arm around my shoulder as I thought I could get. On several other occasions, I've called Al Walker out of the blue, just to ask questions. He's always been kind and available with his wisdom and knowledge. These two gentlemen owed me nothing. Fortunately for me, I was able to get past my own awkwardness and recognize the importance of *picking their brains*.

Initially, I felt that picking someone else's brain seemed a little pushy. Occasionally, it still feels funny. As I began writing this book, I called Dr. Scott Sindelar in Phoenix, Arizona who was already published, to get the inside scoop on writing a book. In a few short words he recommended I purchase a book by Dan Poynter titled, "A Self-Publishing Manual." That piece of information made all the difference in the world. I also called Dr. Sheila Bethel-Murray, who is a very established speaker and author. One fantastic tip she offered was to be patient with the editing. She saved me a lot of unnecessary frustration with that tip alone.

I've come to realize that if you don't ask, you'll never know and opportunities will be gone forever. There are lots of people happy to help, if we just muster the courage to ask. People are like books. I get to learn something from everybody just by *picking their brains*. It's been a very rewarding lesson for me over the last 25 years.

LESSON #54

IS THE PAST HOLDING YOU BACK?

How many of you besides me were brought up during the time that included *threats* if you didn't *clean your plate* because there were starving children in some foreign land? I don't know about you, but the older I get the less I remember of my years as a kid. But this one is like the flashback of the day. Every so often when I'm alone in a restaurant having a salad for lunch, it'll hit me that I've spent five minutes chasing a piece of lettuce around a plate. I then think, "Is this piece of lettuce going to make much of a difference in the big picture?" I feel ridiculous 45 years later when I'm still eating to *clean a plate*. The funny part is that I don't even realize I'm doing it.

As a kid, whenever the "eat your peas or else" threat was issued, my retort was, "Fine, ship the peas to China because I hate peas." Even though I never *bought in* to the clean your plate line, it seems like the line *bought me*. It's never too far below the surface. It makes a great case for how important repetition is for building new habits. Anything repeated enough becomes yours, whether you like it or not.

It seems to me that our past is never too far away and probably closer than we realize. I picture the past like a huge *life magnet* at your back that is almost stronger that you are. As you're trying to make your way through life, there's this tug of war in your head between your magnet and your common sense.

Have you ever heard the ham story? It's the story about a newly married woman who goes to Mom's for dinner. While

153

Mom is preparing the ham, the daughter asks for the first time, "Why do you cut off the end of the ham like that?" Her Mom replies, "Because Grandma did. She's coming over, so let's ask her." Grandma shows up and the granddaughter asks why she cut off the end of the ham before cooking it. Grandma replies, "Oh, you know, in the old days we didn't have the stoves and pans like today, so I would cut off the end so it would fit." You guessed it. Fifty years later we're all still cutting off the end of the ham because Grandma did!

While there are many things we choose to carry with us from our past, we must be mindful of those things that get carried with us for no reason or the reason no longer exists. In the *clean your plate* example, we now live in a world where small portions are recommended, along with leaving something on your plate. There is no longer the emphasis on food like there was in the '50s and '60s.

Carrying the past along with future expectations can be a tremendous burden for anyone. It's important that we be aware of what we can let go so we can make room for different expectations. Here's a funny example. When I grew up my mother changed bed sheets every week. I was shocked the first time I lived away from home and the sheets were not changed weekly. After realizing I wouldn't die, I figured out that there are various reasons for doing things differently. I get a chuckle out of the fact that I practically had to be hit over the head to see it as okay.

During my early career, I remember a speaker recommending that career women cut down on the number of loads of wash they did daily. One idea she gave was to use color-coded towels for each member of the family, so that we could eliminate washing so many towels. I must admit I never would have thought of that on my own. When we're all moving at the speed of light, we're probably just going to do what we've always done. It wasn't until I had time to think about it that it actually made some sense to me. I really wondered if it was doable. I discovered, to my surprise, that it worked fine. No one ever complained. This idea would never have occurred to me. I never would have realized that tiny changes could ease the burden of home and career.

It opened the door for me to start thinking for myself, rather than letting the magnet hold me back and just continue on the path of doing something because I always did or it was all I knew. I've learned that there are many solutions to anything, depending upon the circumstances you face and the goal you want to achieve. What's important to one person is not important to another person at another time, and that's okay. I've found a healthy respect for the past and what I learned, but I have learned to be more open and keep an eye out for that better idea someone else thinks of that will make my life easier.

To this day, with grown children who have been gone for some time, I have had to adjust to the idea of throwing leftovers away. Oh, this is a tough one, but I've come to the conclusion that it looks better in the garbage that it does on me! So, I close my eyes, talk to myself about the benefits of not eating it, and out it goes. Not an easy adjustment when you spent 50 years cleaning your plate. I have learned to catch myself before I pass this stuff along to my grandchildren. I no longer use food as the precursor to something else. There is no punishment if they don't finish. And, so the world turns. Let's be sure we keep the good from the past but leave the unnecessary behind. Let's not allow the magnet of our past to hold us back from embracing the new current thinking of the day. If the new doesn't work, then we can always go back.

LESSON #55

WATCHING OUT FOR SELF-TALK

While it is so easy to blame everyone and everything around us for impeding our ability to function or succeed, this lesson focuses more on how we impede ourselves before others get the chance to do it. We rarely look at it from that perspective.

Our mind is the most powerful computer we will ever work with. What we put into our minds are our thoughts and feelings that will factor into how we behave. Garbage in, garbage out. Positive in, positive out. I'm not sure this is an easy lesson to learn. It's simple enough to understand but not always easy to apply. How we talk to ourselves is critical to our own success. Your level of optimism can come from self-talk. Optimism energizes. If we look around the world we live in, there is no shortage of *martyr* mentality, *poor-me* thinking, or *look-what-I'm-up-against* syndrome. You're either spoon feeding yourself optimism or spoon feeding yourself cynicism.

So, here's a way to start practicing positive self-talk. First, look at the negative symptoms listed on the next page, then check for the positive alternatives. Positive self-talk is like taking vitamins. You won't live forever, but you'll be in the best shape possible. Negative self-talk is like taking poison. It's never a good thing. Remember, nothing works 100% of the time, but positive self talk will always beat the alternative. It's the best way I can think of to protect attitude. Positive attitude is directly connected to enthusiasm and energy for living and working. The good news is that you have a clear choice as to how you talk to yourself.

Negative Symptom (poison)	Positive Alternative (vitamins)
1. Subjective Analysis	1. Objective Analysis
2. Blaming	2. Understanding
3. Too Emotional	3. Logical
4. Revenge	4. Closure
5. Too Critical	5. Tolerance
6. Reactive	6. Proactive
7. Victim Mentality	7. Victor Mentality
8. Compound Problems	8. Solve Problems
9. Complaining	9. Improving
10. Negative Stories	10. Positive Lessons

Oh, by the way, this lesson is not about never having these negative symptoms, but rather about catching ourselves sooner than later from being infected by them. We don't want these negative symptoms to run our lives and outcomes. If we find ourselves miserably caught with a symptom, we need to see what alternative is needed. When I find myself trapped or agonizing over something, I really try to see what positive spin I can put on it. The more we develop our ability to *be optimistic*, the more frequently we will achieve success over unpleasant or negative circumstances. It's about refocusing on possibilities rather than putting our negative magnifying glasses on. It will empower you as a person. Practice enough and you'll be able to help others do the same. This world can always use more optimism and positive self-talk.

This is a wonderful lesson in helping us consider what others see or feel. It can help bring balance to our thinking and provide a healthier mindset when solving life's challenges. It's a great exercise to better understand our weaknesses so we can make more adaptive choices when dealing with other people in our family or at work.

LESSON #56

LET LIFE LEAD YOU A LITTLE BIT

This lesson is about learning to take some risks when trying to be true to yourself. Keep in mind that risk taking and popular opinion are not always compatible. As a matter of fact, I've concluded that when something starts to look a little crazy or unconventional, you just might be on to something new and innovative. Here are some phrases that can work against you: *what we have is fine, it's good enough, let it go, it's not the way we do it,* or my all time favorite, *if it isn't broken then don't fix it.* Let's look at this last one a second. My questions are, how long do we leave it the way it is and who's in charge of making it better? And, why exactly do I have to wait for the world to give me the green light? The phrase implies that we leave it the way it is permanently until we're given permission to think for ourselves.

Here's a story about how life led me to success. When I was growing up, I had a cousin who was five years older than me. In my eyes, she did everything before me. She was pretty, married a successful man, had beautiful children, and lived in a new house. It felt, to me, like she was a hard act to follow. I privately wondered if I could do it. As I recall, our basic options then were to be a secretary or hairdresser unless you "married well." Even marrying well was a challenge because we were all in the same boat of struggling to make ends meet. Lo and behold, I began in the home party plan business in 1972 and asked my cousin if she'd help me by hosting a home party for me. I'll never forget her answer. She said, "Ask me to scrub your floors or babysit your kids, but don't ask me to have a party. Everyone I ever knew who did that didn't make it."

And it hit me. For the first time at age 25, I discovered something she had not accomplished before me. So, skeptically, I decided to take the risk and let this somewhat unconventional opportunity lead me. What I learned about myself, sales, and business was a real eye-opener. For me, it was absolutely like hitting the jackpot. I soon came to realize what a great career fit this was. That first year I was recognized as the number one sales person out of hundreds in the Boston area. Soon I ranked nationally in the top 1% as a sales manager in a field of 12,000 sales managers. I was then promoted to an executive position to build the Western New York area, where I doubled sales in six years and built a multimillion dollar operation. For 20 years, I developed my ability to build business by motivating thousands of people to take action and build winning life habits and lucrative businesses. It was a privilege for me to discover and build new winners. This page wouldn't be long enough to name them all, but they know who they are. Listening to conventional wisdom, these doors would never have been open.

The home party plan business (and there are so many now) remains a very viable and profitable in-home business opportunity for anyone. There is no glass ceiling. It's fun and provides great money, great training, and great products. The two keys to success are using and loving the product and opening the door. It's American entrepreneurship at its finest. I owe my success today to that door I opened in 1972.

The skills I developed on that path have led me for 30 years from sales to professional speaker, trainer and now author. There are two questions I've always asked myself whenever I consider possibilities or take new risks. The first is *what's the worst thing that could happen?* The second question is *can I live with it?* Be open to letting life *lead you* to new opportunity as you paint your own unique masterpiece of success. It could change your life.

LESSON # 57

JUMPING AT OPPORTUNITY

There was a story I heard a long time ago that I've always enjoyed. There once was a young man who was interested in becoming a millionaire. So, one day he asked a millionaire what he needed to do to become a millionaire. The millionaire answered, "Easy. All you have to do is jump at opportunity." The young man was a little puzzled with the answer. So he asked, "Well, that *sounds* easy, but how do I know when opportunity gets here?" The millionaire answered matter-of-factly, "Well you don't. You just have to learn to keep on jumping."

I love this story because not only does it offer hope, it also helps us understand that no one is too big for failure or disappointment. Past accolades, past titles, or years of experience are no guarantee for a straight shot to exactly what we want all the time. I often tell myself that every day I get up I am entitled to only one thing, and that is the experience gained from past successes or failures that serve as my recipe for how to jump today.

This lesson also ties into the "Lowering Your Expectations" lesson. Sometimes we can get too big for our britches and start to think we're pretty comfortable, pretty successful, or on a roll. We must always be mindful of opportunity and taking advantage. I'm a believer in *dabbling in opportunity* rather than giving up your day job totally while you're exploring.

When I started my speaking career, I began dabbling in speaking about 18 months before I left the corporate safety net. While realizing I faced possible transition ahead, I decided it would be on my terms and no one else's terms. I had thought about becoming a professional speaker for several *comfortable* years before corporate changes pushed this dream from the back burner to the front burner.

As a 45-year-old woman facing the prospect of a career transition, I figured I'd be better off building my own business. After all, it's what I did for an international company for 20 years. And once I proved to myself that a speaking career could fly, I made that decision to become a full-time speaker. I knew there would be challenges learning the speaking business, but I was confident I could figure it out. The opportunity for writing this book began 10 years ago. Now here we are many successful opportunities later, and more books yet to come.

Some good news I've discovered is that one successful opportunity typically leads to the next one. Opportunities become connected to create a bigger success. You always want to replace a missed opportunity with a successful one. Never allow disappointment to be the last thing in your memory. Quickly replace it with success.

It's always a good idea to have something to fall back on. Today's workplace and personal challenges don't allow for comfort zones. And just like this lesson illustrates, better it be on your terms than someone else's terms. This was the key to my own successful midlife transition from one career to another. We all have something that is unique to each of us in terms of hobbies, things we do better than most people, or something we have a passion about. Opportunity is as close to us as any of these. A book like this helps us come to terms with the winner within and the opportunities we can take advantage of every day.

Oh, one other thing. Opportunity rarely comes at a convenient time. It can look like it's *in the way* of other things, not very timely, or riddled with obstacles that can make us *think* we can't do it. We can jump and be cautious at the same time. It's like the old saying, "Make sure you have more than one egg in your basket." Another interesting facet about opportunity is that the ones you might *not think* will fly actually do and the ones you *think will* fly may not. It's very important to guard against getting discouraged *before* problem solving or falling into the trap of *if it's meant to be it'll happen.* Having good faith is nice, but not all success comes with that ingredient. Many successes are due to the sheer determination of people with winner thinking.

LESSON #58

THIS PLACE IS LIKE A ZOO

Have you ever thought to yourself, "If everyone thought like me there would be a lot fewer problems in this world"? Well, you're probably not alone on this one. My guess is that most of us have said this to ourselves many times over. This lesson is about giving us a greater understanding of ourselves and those around us, so that we can better adapt and accept that people are probably not going to think like us. One simple reason is that they have a different perspective or agenda they're working to satisfy. Most of us would agree that we're not terribly interested in advancing someone else's agenda more than we advance our own. But, maybe we can cover more than one base at the same time for greater satisfaction on the team.

While in my early years of speaking, I began studying communication styles as part of my programming. I find the topic absolutely fascinating. It allowed me to better understand why certain things occurred. The information helped my awareness for finding solutions that fit the circumstances. Without this information, I often felt like I was playing "pin the tail on the donkey" while blindfolded. I have often wondered why we don't learn this stuff in high school. It's information we almost need *recertification in* every few years.

There are basically four communication styles. While we all are a combination of all four, circumstances play a huge role in what style we adopt given what we face. However, there probably is a primary style we use, with a secondary style not far behind. There are also one or two styles that may drive us crazy. Depending upon what life or the job requires of us,

163

we need to understand our own strengths and weaknesses so we can strengthen those weaknesses to better deal with our circumstances. The four styles include the Driver Style, the Expressive Style, the Amiable Style, and the Analytical Style. While we may behave one way with our kids, families, or workplace, it's entirely possible that we behave very differently under different circumstances. For example, while I'm a driver (bottom line) when working, I'm expressive when speaking or writing, I'm amiable with my grandchildren (no, make that *mush* with my grandchildren), and I'm probably analytical (very detailed) when it comes to organization and time management.

Typically, the Driver and Expressive Styles are extroverts, while the Amiable and Analytical Styles are introverts. The Driver and Analytical Styles are task and goal oriented, while the Expressive and Amiable Styles are people oriented. Already you can see how each style views life from a very different perspective. The driver wants the bottom line in 25 words or less and is all business. The expressive needs and wants interaction to function. The amiable just wants a favorable environment void of confrontation. The analytical is detailed, needs documentation, and views the world from a perspective of safety, quality, and caution.

Now, if you're in driver mode dealing with an analytical you think is holding you up on purpose, you've got the basis for conflict and incompatibility. Drivers, on the other hand, can come across as bulldozers because of their focus on goals, all-business approach, and painful honesty. Incidentally, many situations require driver mode, not the least of which is parenting. We live in a *do-more-with-less* world, so we probably all have to develop our driver style to get the job done without being asked twice. The expressive style is the clever and creative, has lots of ideas, loves to push the envelope, and is a social butterfly. We can disagree with eight out of ten things they say or do, but we tend to like them anyway because of their outgoing approach. The amiable style can be middle of the road and passive. This is the first group that'll be taken advantage of by others. They're seen as good eggs that go along with just about anything rather than fuss. They avoid confrontation like the plague.

Let's talk about some jobs that would adapt to each style. Generals in the Armed Forces and CEOs often are Driver Styles. Sales people, actors, and actresses often are very expressive. Clerical and administrative people are often the Amiable Style. Engineers, doctors, researchers, and computer types often are the Analytical Style.

What's important about this lesson is to understand what style best describes your approach, while gaining insight and understanding into why other styles approach things differently than you do. We need to develop our respect for what each style brings to the team, whether it's a family team, workplace team, or any team we participate in. It also helps us understand where our frustrations come from and, hopefully, how we can accommodate others so that we move better in the same direction, while allowing room for compromise and resolution.

The truth is that any style can drive any other style crazy, given a specific set of circumstances. Let me give you an animal to identify with each style to better understand our "zoo." The dolphin might represent the Amiable Style, the peacock might represent the Expressive Style, the owl would represent the Analytical Style, and the panther would represent the Driver Style. Now, it makes sense that we don't want to treat an owl like a peacock, or a dolphin like a black panther. The advantage is that each animal brings different traits that we need on any team.

Each style will provide a different perspective to consider whenever solutions or decisions need to be made. It illustrates the need to factor in beforehand the views and positions of each style by dealing with issues and conflict upfront, before implementing a solution or decision. This approach will reduce unnecessary conflict and greatly enhance the outcome. Used successfully, it'll provide for planning and the prevention of unnecessary stress. Whether in a family or workplace, this knowledge goes a long way in building a healthy team. We need to understand our own strengths and weaknesses first. Then we can understand and appreciate the strengths and weaknesses of others.

We may live in a zoo, but let's get back to respecting our differences. They provide great balance when used positively.

LESSON #59

CONTROL THE CONTROLLABLE AND COPE WITH THE UNCONTROLLABLE

This lesson serves as a wonderful coping strategy. Have you ever felt like it's one step forward and two steps back? Have you ever been part of change or growth that can make you feel that things are just spinning out of control? Ever experience times where it just feels like things are getting away from you? Most of us can certainly identify with these statements. They can be symptoms of a negative shifting focus, especially if we are dealing with challenges, changes, or new and unknown territory.

One lesson I learned several years ago that can help redirect focus to being productive rather than frustrated and stressed, is to control the controllable and cope with the uncontrollable. Sometimes we don't even know what the cause is. Finding a solution can seem impossible. I have come to recognize and call this feeling "discombobulated." They're the times when you just want to stop the world and get off. During those times I've experienced this negative pull, I have found that tiny changes can make a huge difference. I'm sure you've heard the phrase "the devil is in the details." So, here are some tips and techniques that can help sort the good from the bad to help regain personal power and focus on what we can control. More often than not, it's been my experience that tiny changes make huge differences. Let's find them together.

Take a piece of paper and draw a vertical line down the middle. On one side write the word *uncontrollable*. On the other side, write the word *controllable*. First, begin with the uncontrollable side and jot down whatever feels uncontrollable. Usually, if you're frustrated there's no problem filling in this side. The list can include things like too much work, not enough help, always rushing, no time to myself, not enough sleep, forgetting things, not enough time, and too much stress. Try being specific about what seems uncontrollable. Then write down what feels controllable. It's a way of identifying successes to play back in your own head. You may even experience difficulty jotting anything down on the controllable side. This is probably a symptom of losing personal power and not taking control of a negative situation for too long.

The goal then is to try to identify, from the uncontrollable list, at least one or two items that you can bring under control. Do the easiest one first to achieve fast relief. What happens here is that you begin identifying your sources of frustration or stress. You develop a picture that will help you prioritize and identify which items you can begin to control better. It's a to-do list for yourself. I always recommend training seminars if specific skill areas, like time management or organization, are lacking. Sometimes just speaking to someone you respect can help you identify simple solutions. It's a way of identifying what *step one* is and where you can begin to reverse that downward spiral you're on. Once you begin focusing on solutions one item at a time, you have begun the reversal process. What happens then is that because you have redirected your focus to making small, simple, and easy improvements, you will be better able to cope with what may indeed be uncontrollable (circumstances beyond your control).

A two-year-old can be an example of circumstances beyond your control. Their ability to communicate well with an adult is usually 12 to 18 months off. Focusing on what you can control will help you better deal with what you can't control. Having teenagers who respond with one or two word answers also falls into the category of circumstances beyond your control. Learning to deal with these in a positive way will help you communicate better and feel better. Let's face it, in both cases we must continue to communicate. It will take awareness and problem solving to put a positive spin on your word choices and communication.

Control the controllable and you'll cope better with the uncontrollable. Frequently, we don't effectively solve problems because we haven't developed the proper awareness to put things in perspective. Once we have good and accurate awareness, then problem solving can occur. Frustration can often be a sign that we have mounting challenges or problems that we are not solving as we go. Therefore we begin to get overwhelmed and start feeling somewhat hopeless. This is a wonderful exercise to help us move forward, rather than continuing that sinking feeling.

Very often solutions come from reorganizing something, implementing a change, or respecting our time enough to stop being all things to all people. I remember a time when I was a sales manager at the top of my game and my goal was to get home in time for my children arriving from school. As great an idea as this was, the rest of the world discovered it was the best time to reach me. So I got caught with a ringing phone 30 times from 3 PM to 6 PM, while trying to coordinate my children's activities. I felt like I was being pulled in ten different directions. So, when I got to the point that a ringing phone brought on feelings of nausea, I decided to turn off the ringer for those three hours. My answering machine let people know that I would return calls between 6 PM and 6:45 PM. I can't begin to tell you what tremendous relief I got just from making that tiny change. It took two minutes to implement. I got three uninterrupted hours with my family and a breather for myself by compartmentalizing the phone calls. It was like achieving freedom in my own home. It worked like a charm.

Had I not solved this annoying problem, it would not have been too long before I started telling myself that, yes, careers and family are really not compatible. Remember, we must be on guard for the frustration that can shut down our problem solving skills at a time when we need them most.

What's been amazing to me is how effective an exercise like this one can be to "taking charge" of your emotional intelligence to deal with the fast-paced world we live in. If we can catapult ourselves back into a better quality of life, then why not do it? The alternative is certainly not something we should settle for. Are we talking about a higher level of functioning? You bet we are! It's teachable and learnable in our quest to live and think like winners when less than winning circumstances find us.

LESSON #60

GET EXCITED ABOUT SOMETHING

Many years ago, one speaker taught that when you can't get needs met from the outside, you need to turn within yourself to get your needs met. It supports the notion that you must first be happy with yourself to find happiness in the world.

I've learned that when you are satisfied that you did everything in your power to achieve something, you will then be better able to accept the outcome and move on. I've come to appreciate that doing your best is a key to acceptance and resetting goals without getting stuck in the muck of discouragement. It's understanding the learning curve and discovery phase of achievement. It can bring closure to what doesn't go the way we intended. It'll protect you "within" when you're dealing with life's ups and downs.

One thing I share with audiences is that each of us needs to be aware of what we are excited about both personally and professionally. When I ask the question, "What are you excited about personally?" people often find themselves scratching their heads and wondering what the answer might be. We need to be able to answer that question to ourselves on a daily basis. Every day we need to look forward to and be excited about something, especially when the day can size up to be a stressful one. Personally, I get excited about good health, conversations with friends, flowers budding, springtime, sunshine, seeing my grandchildren, talking to my kids and husband, unwinding, quiet time for myself, putting my mind in neutral, winner thinking, and making life moments special. My list could go on and on.

When asking the question, "What are you excited about professionally?" typically I get the look "huh?" For me, being excited professionally means being the very best I can be, figuring out what my next move is, opening a new customer door, giving someone information that helps them, turning on life's light bulbs for people, learning from my audiences, and just the satisfaction of knowing I'm giving back to people what others have given me over the years. It's important that we all have a sense of purpose for why we do whatever we do. Dr. Victor Frankl, whom I mentioned earlier in the book, refers to this as step one to giving life meaning. Hopefully, I've translated this notion into real application for our day-to-day success in giving our individual lives meaning. When we can't get from without, we must get from within. When Dr. Frankl was a prisoner in a World War II concentration camp in Germany, he certainly had to depend on "within" when he couldn't get from without (his surroundings). Most of us will never deal with this level of challenge, but we certainly can learn a lesson from it.

One exercise I like to recommend for a family dinner or get-together is to have everyone at the table, one at a time, tell what they're excited about for that day. Start with the younger children. You'll be amazed at how they help bring our adult focus back to being excited about something daily. As a matter of fact, your kids might have a week's worth lined up in advance, while the parents are still scratching their heads to come up with something. So, go ahead, and start thinking about what you're excited about each day. It's a great approach to buffer yourself from life's challenges and disappointments and allow yourself to turn within for happiness you might not find on the outside. Don't expect from others what you need to find within yourself. Learn to create your own focus of excitement about life, relationships, and the workplace. It's a very good thing.

LESSON #61

POSITIVES BUILD ENERGY
NEGATIVES DRAIN ENERGY

This lesson ties in with positive self-talk in Lesson 55. If you listen to the world around us, it's incredible how often we hear negative feedback. We can all fall into that trap and it's important to learn better and more positive habits. I've certainly recognized that, for many of us, negative motivation drains energy rather than builds it. You don't have to look far for examples of negative motivation. Calling a young child a bad boy or a bad girl. Telling teenagers that they're slow, stupid, sloppy, careless, thoughtless, or anything else, confirms our eagerness to critique and ridicule. Sadly, we learn it from people around us. I'm not sure we realize how much it can drain people's energy for trying.

Our goal should always be to bring out the best in others. One approach we can take when communicating is to allow for what we didn't see, information they didn't know or understand clearly, and their focus or view of things that may be different from ours. In Lesson 58, we learned the different styles people use. We learned that some people are focused on being safe, being cautious, and not making mistakes. They might be perceived as slow and holding up the works when, in fact, they are approaching something from a quality control standpoint. Some people focus on a favorable environment and would do anything to maintain calmness. They might be perceived as middle of the road and passive. Some people focus on socialization as a way to lighten up and cope. They might be perceived as airheads or timewasters. Some people focus on bottom line and getting results. They might be perceived as controlling and unfriendly. If any of these styles don't match our current style, then we tend to toss in some negative comment, rather than positively communicate so we can all move in the same direction.

I guess it comes down to believing in people and expecting their cooperation *before* we get annoyed. Typically in supervisory programs, one technique is to always deal with a situation immediately rather than waiting. The closer the coaching is to the situation at hand, the better the outcome. More often than not we wait too long, let frustrations and inaccurate perceptions grow, and then overreact.

I learn great lessons being with my two grandsons. It allows me to practice some of my techniques. It's amazing to me that when I take a positive "coaching" approach with the children, I usually get pretty good cooperation. Negative words, shame, or negative critique usually bring on hurt feelings, fear, and embarrassment, all of which drain energy for whatever we're trying to accomplish.

Have you ever heard this one? "Hello, my name is BAD DOG. What's yours?" If people audiotaped what they hear us say, conversation after conversation, would it be perceived as positive or negative? Fear, resistance, and inadequacy are bred from negative motivation. That comes from following rather than leading and it tends to be reactive. Positive motivation comes from planning, coaching, caring, patience, and expectation in a productive way. I learned from Dr. Roger Firestien about a study done in education about the *praise to criticism ratio*. The recommendation for maintaining behavior was *four praise statements for every criticism*. The recommendation for changing behavior was *eight praise statements for every criticism*. This study certainly supports my observations about building winners. Influencing people is always more powerful than antagonizing people to get cooperation.

Coaching through positive reinforcement is the *technique of choice* for influencing others to succeed. I'll take the *build-me-up* approach any day over the *knock-me-down* approach. Certainly, from a coaching perspective, it's always important to show people their past successes, achievements, and capabilities when delivering any critique, so you can help them buy into their own ability and potential. Showing others what *they* have to gain as a result of positive change is a key to *selling* anything, whether it's an idea, advice, product, or service.

It's *so* easy to deliver negatives. Maybe in doing so we unconsciously give ourselves importance and greater value. Taking a positive approach is always more productive. It takes more patience, thought, and planning, but is more likely to help us arrive at our destination to assure closure, understanding, and redirection. Positive motivation prevents *foot in mouth disease* and allows us the opportunity to give *the benefit of the doubt*. Incidentally, the more we *give the benefit of the doubt*, the more likely people will award it back to us in our time of need. Negative motivation puts us in a *holier than thou light* and can simply set us up for critique by those we motivate negatively. We all need to remember this advice. It's a lesson we may know but need to reconsider frequently to be sure we're playing our cards the right way.

For me personally, it's very important to focus on the positives in life rather than the negatives. One technique would be to *quickly* replace a negative with a positive to help put the negative behind us. I'd rather look at any negative from a distance rather than wallow in it. Sometimes if we don't feel like winners, there is a human tendency to display our negatives to the world, to show ourselves off as victims. Our goal should be to focus on successes and pursuit of our *next* success. In sales, I always remember the perspective of dealing with the *no* by telling yourself that each *no* puts you closer to the next *yes*. It worked then and it works now.

Starting today replace negatives with positives for a healthier inner self. In doing so, you create a more positive outward approach when interacting with others. If you're one of those people who were standing behind the door when God passed out patience, then this is probably something you can relate to. This is one of those lessons that may be understood very well but needs to be reviewed as a reminder of its power and importance. It's important to make a daily commitment to help this world be a better place by using this very powerful tool. Positive reinforcement and positive motivation build people in the right direction which is UP!

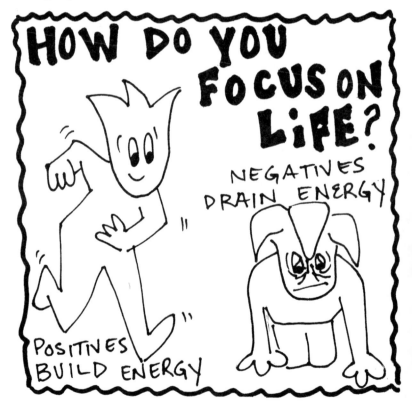

LESSON #62

KINDS OF SUCCESS

I like defining success in five different categories as I observe the winners around me. The five categories of success include *easy success*, *tragic success*, *tough success*, *happy success*, and *choice success*. I've discovered that we will all, at one time or another, be challenged with each during a lifetime. It's so easy to watch the Super Bowl or the Olympics and see success in a competitive way. But, more often than not, in the Game of Life we are competing with ourselves to succeed against the odds and obstacles we face. There's no big award ceremony or trophy being handed to you. Perhaps the world will never know or care of your struggle, problems, and success.

What's most important in this lesson is that we each personally recognize the importance of winning without a cheering section or recognition. Our real success and victories come from within and personal achievement. So let's consider the different kinds of success.

First, there's the easy success. That's the kind of success where something just falls into place with no real challenges. It's purely coincidental and more of a fate kind of thing that just falls into your lap. For me, that kind of success happens if some speaker cancels at the last minute, the meeting planner goes to the National Speakers Association's website, and up my name comes as being the closest to the event. That's what I call a "gimme." It was a process that brought about a success that was literally handed to me. Our mistake is that we start depending on easy successes because they *do* happen occasionlly *or* we start thinking we deserve them for one reason or another.

Second, there's tragic success. That's the kind of success where people survive very difficult circumstances and live to tell about it. I'd put POWs in this category. People who don't see themselves as heroes but the rest of the world does. We've all heard stories of athletes who've had terrible accidents and come back, to the amazement of the medical community. One speaker named W. Mitchell, *the man who wouldn't be defeated*, survived a terrible fire. As a result, he was very disfigured and disabled and was confined to a wheelchair. His story is incredible! His story puts challenges in perspective. His ability to tell it and be funny blows your mind. His is a tremendous story of hope and success after tragedy. He set new standards for what human beings are capable of achieving.

Third, there's the tough success. That's the kind of success that doesn't come easily. It's the kind of success you're going to have to fight for. It can be born from a life or death situation. Stopping smoking can be a tough success and tougher for some than others. Losing weight can be a tough success and tougher for some than others. Alcoholism and drug addiction fall into this category, as well. I remember when my Dad successfully dealt with his alcoholism at age 40 (he's now 80). He became so sick and tired of being sick and tired, literally, that he made a choice one *not-so-fine day* to put it behind him and start anew. When you really think about it, he had to stop doing something he loved doing 20 times every single day. That's not easy. I have difficulty giving up Twinkies when I want to lose a few pounds. It's hard to believe that Twinkies can dominate your mind when you can't have them. I've always said that my Dad's experience was the first time that I learned about achieving success against the odds. I'm very proud and thankful that he was able to pull it off. Believe me, our family, at the time, was probably more pitied than applauded. With just one short relapse, he made it happen and turned away from the bottle forever. Even more remarkably, he loved and embraced his new life as he learned he had the ability to influence others with the same problem. I've come to see my Dad as an *instrument of peace*. When you think about it, who's better suited to help other alcoholics than the former alcoholic? Of course, my Dad is now considered an old-timer in AA. I remember him saying one day, as he was comparing his days as a drinker to today's drinkers, "I used to *spill* more than they drink." Fortunately, the standards for seeking treatment have changed for the positive. The good news is that I can find the humor in his statement 40 years later because I was able to observe his incredible success and rebirth as a human being. It helped me see the value of strength and courage in my family. It helped me see my family in a winning light. I learned we had the stuff it takes to succeed through tough success.

Fourth, there's the happy success. That's the kind of success we can enjoy from someone else. For example, my grandchildren are a happy success. I think of it like enjoying my own children again with one big and critical difference: they go home to great babysitters, their parents. I can be the weekend hero and enjoy the good part with little or no responsibility. My husband and I are a fun part of their lives and they're a fun part of ours. This success wouldn't have been born unless I raised my own family. So, this can really be what you gain down the line after putting in the effort to make something happen either personally or at work. Happy success is watching the people you lead succeed even better than you succeeded. Happy success for me is anytime someone in my audience tells me that something I said changed their life or business. Happy success is doing something nice for someone else that you didn't have to do. It could be inviting people to a get-together for no special reason. Happy success is every time we improve an outcome over the average bear approach.

Fifth, there's the choice success. That's the kind of success you choose for yourself. For me it was my choice to become an entrepreneur in 1972, and later to become a professional speaker in 1990, to share what I've been so fortunate to learn in my career. It's any time we stretch out of our comfort zone to make one of our dreams a reality. It's putting something where there's nothing. It's changing the course of history for your family. It's opening your own doors of opportunity. It's learning all you can from whomever you can. It's making a difference in the world we live. It's leaving a legacy in the wake of your life. It's about taking a stand to make necessary changes. It's about being heard to improve outcomes. It's about caring. I remember one secretary who worked for me many years. Pam was wonderful. Pam could be counted on to finish my sentences. She learned and cared about how I thought and she did an outstanding job supporting my objectives. One day I asked Pam, "Why are you so good and some people never figure that out?" I'll never forget her simple four-word answer, "You have to *care*." Pam was one of those special people in my life experience that I consider to be a choice success. She made a choice to succeed each and every day. Hats off to winners! I love 'em!

You see, we need to feel good about our approach to success and all the different circumstances under which we will be challenged to succeed. Our goal then becomes rising to the occasion as a winner by taking the higher road of human functioning and by taking advantage of the potential in our treasure chest. People have proven over and over again that they possess a marvelous ability to overcome and succeed. No one was *standing behind the door* when God passed that out!

LESSON #63

LIFE TEACHES YOU TWO THINGS: WHAT YOU WANT AND WHAT YOU DON'T WANT

Don't you just hate making mistakes or missing something you should have taken advantage of? How about when you observe others do the same thing? Don't you wish you could tell people and they'd just plain take your word for something? Ever notice how people who finally stop smoking almost become evangelists to the masses who haven't figured it out yet? These people go from chain smoker to preacher almost overnight once they get their *wake-up call.*

One thing for sure is we all learn some things the hard way. *Doubting Thomas* didn't just exist in the Bible. I think we all have a *Doubting Thomas* side. Most of us don't accept information or advice the first time it gets delivered. Rather we question it, pull it apart, look for deception or ulterior motives, or just plain discount it.

Incidentally, ever notice how we're less critical of our own *mistakes* than we are of the *mistakes* of others that take their toll on *our* lives? It's the old armchair quarterback approach of "I'll tell you what they ought to do if they were *smart.*" Or, "Why don't you just stop doing such and such?" The answer is pretty much for the same reason *we* don't stop doing something we need to stop doing. We may lack awareness, we may think it's no big deal, or we may think it's not going to happen to us. Maybe we see it as a remote problem compared to other problems.

We can learn great lessons from how children learn. They learn by repetition and stories told in testimonial fashion. So, even if they haven't had some particular *story* happen to them, the story sets the stage for them to be prepared in case it does. One day my grandchildren were watching a children's television program called *Little Bill*. The show was about one child calling Little Bill names. The dad helps Little Bill deal with it by saying to the name-caller, "So?" Just last week, one of my grandsons came to tell me someone had said something negative to him and he was hurt. I reminded him of Little Bill saying, "So?" from the show. Immediately his little face broke into a smile because he remembered the story. My reminder gave him what he needed to better approach his dilemma. It allowed him to stop focusing on something that isn't true by starting to focus on how to deal with it. Don't give importance to something that's not important.

Life teaches us two things. One, of course, is that we learn from what happens to us personally. No question about it, when we learn a hard lesson, we <u>never</u> unlearn it. Hard lessons stay a long time! The other way we learn is by looking around and observing the world around us. Think of it as life's *programming* for adults.

It's occurred to me many times over the years how much I've learned and applied simply by observing others. Winners learn to develop the ability to gain wisdom by observation rather than by the proverbial wake-up call. I'm not sure we have to get *hit in the face with a pie* when we can <u>avoid</u> the *pie in the face* by simply watching others. This lesson can provide a much softer landing than the hard lessons we learn from wake-up calls.

Your upbringing, for example, will teach you what you do *not* want to duplicate and what you *do* want to duplicate, just by taking stock of how you felt and learning from it. It helped me discover the person I wanted to be. It was a character building experience that has given my life depth and meaning. It has helped me keep a level of humility anytime I think I'm getting too big for my britches. It has helped me develop compassion for others and good problem solving skills. This lesson shows that we can develop a healthy respect for tough times, walk away a better person for having been exposed to them, and help others along the way.

Our tendency, of course, is to say, "It's not fair. Why me? I don't deserve this." Success can come when we define in a positive way what we want and what we don't want. The definition of who we are is sometimes achieved by process of elimination. "I want that, I don't want that, I want that, and I don't want that, that, and that." This lesson ties in with the lesson that difficulty can be *the springboard to success*. The human spirit can come back from tremendous challenge. It's a lesson that can serve us well and one I'm grateful for learning. It's a lesson I wish everyone could learn because it holds the key to successfully dealing with difficulty that is put upon us by others or brought on by ourselves. Perfection doesn't exist. Making boo-boos does. It's the old lesson of "turning lemons into lemonade." And, you know what, lemonade is a whole lot better than lemons, right?

LESSON #64

KAIZEN

Ever heard the word *Kaizen*? I first heard it a number of years ago from a bank president I was working with. He passed it along to me and I was so grateful for a word that identified the passion we develop to improve outcomes and results. Kaizen is actually a Japanese word for "the theory of continuous improvement." It becomes even more meaningful when you consider how the Japanese applied the theory to their economic advantage after World War II. While I was born right after the war, I remember growing up seeing these cheaply made Japanese do-dads. I still can see the thin gold label with the words "Made in Japan" on it. At the time, that label sure didn't stand for quality. It represented quite the opposite.

If you think about the devastation that Japan faced after World War II, it's amazing how they turned their country *on a dime* from producing cheap do-dads to setting the standards for excellence in technology and automobile manufacturing. It's been long enough now that Japan's image of cheap do-dads is all but history to those of us who can remember it.

Kaizen, the theory of continuous improvement, means that no matter how good something is, we are <u>personally</u> committed to making it better and better as we strive for excellence. Kaizen doesn't *watch* what others do. Kaizen *creates the standards* others follow. It allows for the individual thinking that connects to change and progress. For example, if you do something you've never done before and you feel pretty good about getting it up and running at 80%, Kaizen means that you want to remain committed to upgrade to the highest level. Let's suppose, on the other hand, that you've been doing something very well for a long time and you're pretty happy with it. Let's say it's at 95%. Kaizen means that we are on the lookout to improve the 95% to 96% to 97%, and so on. At this point, of course, it doesn't mean new discoveries every day. What it does mean is that we must remain *open to possibility* as circumstances become conducive to improving our approach, process, or outcome. It's the energy and excitement we build when we discover innovative ways to save or shave time, improve results, or find a faster and better way to accomplish something or improve the quality of our lives or work.

My question to you is, "What improvements have you made to your personal or professional life in the last month?" If you're puzzled right now, then it may be because you can't really think of anything or it's hard to come up with something unless you go back a long time. This lesson teaches that you, like the Japanese, *can turn the tide* to success any time you choose if you apply Kaizen. It's like *life's scavenger hunt* to search for missing puzzle pieces to your masterpiece.

Applying Kaizen is the *take-charge victor mentality* that really replaces the victim mentality. It's the art of tuning ourselves in to possibility, taking risks, trying new things, and getting excited about our own discoveries and upgrades, rather than settling for status quo or good enough. It always feels good when we discover something first before others do. It's a great ego booster.

As I reflect on the last 50 years, the Japanese have done an incredible job of building their country and changing their course of history for the better. If it can work for a country over a relatively short period of time, then it can certainly work for the individual who learns the principle of Kaizen.

It's a great example of learning by looking around our world, identifying a great idea, and putting it to work for us without first getting a wake-up call. Softer landings are always preferred over *wake-up calls*. Improving life on your terms is always the preferred choice.

So, think about what you can get excited about and what you'd like to see improved. Then, put on your Kaizen thinking cap. The sky's the limit for winners!

LESSON #65

DO WHAT MATTERS
NOT JUST WHAT SHOWS

Here's a great story that has inspired me. It's about a man who rents a home by the ocean to write. Every morning when he wakes up, he notices a boy on the beach who seems to be repeating the same movement over and over again. The man became curious. So, one morning he walked down to the beach to get a closer look. The closer he got, he could see that the boy was picking up starfish that had washed up on to the beach that morning and was throwing them back into the ocean. He then realized that the boy got up early every day to do the same thing. As the man reached the boy, he mentioned that he'd seen him out every morning and inquired about what he was doing on the beach. The boy explained that he was throwing the starfish back into the sea. The man asked the boy what difference it would make, because the beach went on for miles and starfish wash up on to the beach every day. The boy patiently leaned over to pick up another starfish and then, as he tossed it into the sea, he said, *"It makes a difference to this one."*

There is no traffic jam on the extra mile. Making a little dent in a big problem can be seen as pie in the sky or fantasyland. This lesson is about the winner thinking it takes to follow something through because it matters, not just because there's a prize or recognition. It's our ability to do something because *we can* rather than focus on whether someone deserves it or not or we like them or not. It's about integrity to do the right thing at the right time. It's about standing for something that no one else may care about.

One example of this lesson was Mavis Leno's focus on the plight of women in Afghanistan during Taliban rule. She laid the groundwork for world awareness of something that didn't particularly affect any of us. Because she kept hope alive for years without the world taking great notice, the plight of Afghan women became a cause that has affected women all over the world. It's so easy to accept that *that's the way it is* and think we can't help change the world. Another shining example of doing what matters is John Walsh, who has campaigned for missing children ever since he lost his own child. He was an everyday working man, thrown into an unknown situation, who went on to help improve the outcomes for other families.

Unlikely heroes are everywhere. It is indeed a courageous person who steps up to the plate to begin the long journey of tossing *one starfish at a time* into the sea, although the sea may go on for miles and miles with no end in sight. Doing what matters and going the extra mile are roles we all get to play as we build a better world for those who come after us.

LESSON #66

THE HAVES AND THE HAVE-NOTS

Growing up in the '50s, I recall hearing things like, "We don't have much, but we eat good," "People with money just have problems," "Being happy is all that matters," and "You ought to see how much they give you at such and such a restaurant." One childhood memory I have was going to an Italian restaurant to celebrate my grammar school graduation. Right then and there I decided I liked restaurants. A couple of years later, as a sophomore, someone invited me to his senior prom. It was the very first time I went to a *fancy* restaurant. I clearly remember panicking because I had no idea what to do. I didn't know what *a la carte* meant and I didn't know how to order. I didn't know different salad dressing names and I remember feeling scared and uncomfortable with the whole thing. It was one time when *happy* should have been enough, I suppose, but it wasn't.

What I lacked was experience. I was very naïve about how the world worked and what possibilities existed. I guess you could say I didn't know what I didn't know. I've discovered, to my absolute delight, that life offers so much that is so exciting. In those days, when I would wonder why some people seemed to have *stuff* but we didn't have *stuff*, I remember concluding that's just the way it was. Too bad! It never occurred to me until I was in my 20s that I could change the status quo.

Once I got a taste of business opportunity and success and began to build on my own potential, I was amazed at the doors of opportunity that began opening for me and my family. I started to get a taste of what it was like to have stuff!

And, what do ya know? I discovered that whatever problems we had, they were better solved because of knowledge, opportunity, and financial security. I realized what I had been missing all along.

I remember when my daughter was in high school in a rather affluent Western New York community. She came home one day and said, "You know, Mom, everybody at school has goals and I like that." And I said, "I like it too, honey." Kids know the difference between the *haves* and the *have-nots*. I certainly did. My daughter certainly did.

While both groups may seem at odds, I've discovered some real similarities between both sides of this economic coin. Incidentally, I like the *haves* side better. What I've discovered is that the *have-nots* want it all just like everybody else. They give it all they've got, just like everybody else. On the other hand, the *haves* want it all and they give it all they've got just like everybody else, too. The basic difference is that the *have-nots*, while giving it all they've got, don't quite give enough to make a difference and have no clue what's missing. So, the odds continue to be stacked against them. The *haves*, on the other hand, put in everything they've got (for example, awareness and knowledge), but they tend to put in *more*. So, while there are no guarantees of success for anyone, the odds are stacked *in* their favor for getting more of what they want more of the time.

Picture the *have-nots* stretching out their arms in front of themselves to illustrate how much is *put in*. Now picture the *haves* stretching their arms way behind their backs to illustrate how much *more* can be *put in*. Therein lies a huge difference. Despite their efforts, the *have-nots* lack the resources to stack the odds in their own favor. If they do succeed, it can be a *slip through the cracks* type of success. We can make life easier. Why struggle more than we have to?

The *have-nots* can become *haves,* but to accomplish this they need to work especially hard to *fill in the blanks* and find what they need to put in to succeed.

Now, everybody certainly deserves to choose whatever life is right for them. At the same time, I believe everyone deserves to know *what it takes* to achieve whatever anyone else can achieve. I simply want to help remove that *mysterious wondering* that we can carry with us throughout our lives. Fortunately, for more than a quarter billion of us in the United States, we already have so much in our favor. However, that leaves us with the responsibility to make things happen for ourselves.

Whenever we want something the first step is to believe in possibility and the second step is to fill in the blanks by turning on one light bulb at a time. It's good old-fashioned pioneering, and this country was built on the backs of pioneers. Let's avoid getting caught in the *rich get richer mentality,* which implies we're stuck. Let's check our treasure chest, put one foot in front of the other, and learn everything we can so that we become the best we possibly can be!

We *all* want it all. We *all* want happiness. We just need to learn what ingredients are missing that would make the difference and stack the odds in our favor to personal victory. And, if no one ever told you *you can do it,* then I will. You can do it!

LESSON #67

IT FEELS FUNNY

The question is, "How do you perceive change?" "It feels funny," you say? Well, the good news in this lesson is that any change is always going to feel funny, awkward, and deliberate until we move to a new comfort zone. This lesson is about having hope and believing in our ability to navigate successfully through change. Have you ever heard, *when one door closes, another opens but, man, these hallways are the pits*? Transition is rarely pretty but certainly doable. This lesson helps in developing coping skills.

When I was in my early 20s, the Catholic Church decided to make some changes. One of the changes at Mass included having the people turn and greet each other with a "peace be with you" greeting toward the end of Mass. Honestly, as I think back, it's almost hard for me to believe people made such a big deal about this tiny change. There was a point in the Mass when the priest would turn to the congregation and say, "Peace be with you." Formerly it meant *grab your keys, you're outta here*. Then the Church decided that the congregation should turn to those around them, shake hands, and wish each other "peace be with you." I remember the older generation commenting on how ridiculous they thought this was. Keep in mind that this was still at a time when many people were not comfortable shaking hands with friends, much less with people they didn't know. I started to believe, like everyone else, that this was unnecessary and they should leave it alone. Anyway, as this new ritual rolled out, it was really funny observing people trying to decide how long they could get away with *ignoring* the new change. Some people still stood like soldiers as if to say, "This is stupid and if enough of us ignore it, they'll give up this ridiculous idea." The awkwardness was very apparent. This example is only funnier because these were the children of God in the House of God, unable to accept this change for years.

As we fast-forward many years, I've noticed that all the grumbling over this tiny change has long since passed. What has happened is that people have grown quite comfortable with this fellowship approach. It gives my heart such pleasure to see people really extend themselves to include anyone around them. This tiny change in the Mass actually helped elevate the social skills of people at that time. It took people a very long time to adjust. Today this example seems ridiculous because people have become quite comfortable shaking hands. That was not always the case.

What I've learned over the last 30 years is that change *always* feels funny initially. Then, at some point down the road, it doesn't feel funny at all. What it tells me today, though, is how much responsibility we have when we are 50ish to become positive role models to the younger generation as we deal with world changes. Even the tiniest changes can throw people for a loop. We do have a responsibility to use logic and coping skills to facilitate and influence positively. How *we* react to something gives hopefulness or hopelessness to those watching and learning. Change is progress that feels funny but we shouldn't let awkwardness prevent us from embracing the unknown. It's also a great lesson in adaptability and flexibility that go hand-in-hand with believing in our own ability and potential.

LESSON #68

ARE YOU TIRED OR ARE YOU BORED?

Picture that you're in your house, exhausted, mumbling, and feeling a little bad for yourself. You're feeling kind of hopeless and wondering if it's all worth it. Ever happen to you? Now, imagine that at that same moment, the Prize Patrol shows up after the Super Bowl and knocks on your front door to make you the Publishers Clearing House's newest millionaire. Would you agree that your outlook would definitely do a 180 turnaround at that moment? All of a sudden, fatigue is gone. You have just found energy you didn't know you had. You don't sleep for days because of the excitement of it all.

Well, needless to say, winning a million dollars is going to be out of reach for the masses, but this lesson is not. This lesson is about understanding that *we* possess the ability to change our own minds any time we want to if we're feeling like life has lost its excitement and has been replaced with fatigue, boredom, or burnout.

Sometimes we don't recognize the symptoms of boredom or burnout for what they are. I believe they're the human way of alerting us that life needs a boost, a change, or some excitement to reignite our own spark. I think we need to just get excited about something to divert our attention away from being *sad sacks*. I have often wondered if unhappiness comes more from a sense of being unfulfilled in our personal achievement, contribution to life, and value to ourselves. Sometimes our treasure chest becomes a bench we lie down on because we're tired.

It's especially at times like these that we may need to push ourselves into new ventures or adventures. I've frequently recommended that people take advantage of community continuing education classes. They offer lots of easy, fun, and inexpensive activities and classes. Aside from being someone's spouse or parent, we are *individuals first* and we need to nurture our own individuality. I wonder if sometimes our individuality gets lost for too long in the agendas of others.

We must hold strong to the belief that excitement about life comes from within. Whatever excitement comes from the outside (for example, spouses, children, and work) is just the icing on the cake. We must first be happy with ourselves and be mindful that we have the power to reignite our excitement about life rather than just linger in fatigue, boredom, or burnout. In case the Prize Patrol doesn't show up at your house, you can get that adrenalin flowing by finding excitement in your life!

LESSON #69

LOOK AT THE SMALL PICTURE
AND THE BIG PICTURE

Sometimes I wonder if we give value to the day-to-day commitment we make to the big picture of events. It's about connecting the dots of successful little day-to-day pictures that go into making a lifelong successful big picture possible.

This lesson is about making every day count to be the best we can possibly be. Doing the little things right and well consistently will always add up to your *best foot forward* approach. The big picture always begins with the seemingly unimportant day-to-day tasks or decisions that we may not take very seriously or think add up to very much.

These days, technology is a great example for how people prepare for the future. We can be first in line or dead last and struggling to catch up to what everyone else has if we've missed the boat. Education is a piece of the little picture that eventually helps form the big picture for how we provide for our future and families. Over the years, more and more women have recognized the importance of being independent by acquiring the ability to take care of themselves financially and having something to fall back on if they choose. Retirement has become a much greater big picture for today's generation. More and more people are saving earlier for their future after retirement. It's an area that has really gotten a lot of needed attention. Employers and retirement plans have made this a much more significant priority today. This big picture is real for many more people than it was years ago.

We should ask ourselves, "Is what I'm doing today helping

me to advance toward my goals for the future?" We need to connect our *today* with our *tomorrow,* rather than take it as it comes as if magically some master plan will emerge by itself.

Often we hear people ask us where we want to be in five or ten years. We must know what those answers are and do what's necessary day-to-day to best position ourselves for that big picture. Keeping our eyes open and assessing our direction are always good strategies to stay on course. Remember in the story of Alice in Wonderland, when Alice comes upon the Cheshire cat and asks which way to go? The cat asks her where she wants to go and she replies that she doesn't know. So, the cat tells her that it probably doesn't matter which way she goes if she has no specific destination. The way we choose to go today will always connect to where we end up tomorrow.

LESSON #70

LEARN TO RISE ABOVE

Can you remember being teased as a kid? Maybe it was by another sibling or someone else. I remember being teased by my brother all the time. My mother would give the typical parent response, "Don't look at him." And I would do the typical kid thing by continuing to focus on him, which would make it worse. I remember thinking how absolutely impossible it seemed to *stop* looking at him. It was *so easy* to get sucked in to someone else *egging* us on. To me it felt impossible to avoid. I wondered why my mother would offer such *lame* advice.

Truth is, this is one of those lessons I call *simple but not easy,* because it's hard to apply. However, the goal is to rise above whenever possible. Maybe we won't be successful as often as we'd like, but this is clearly one of those successes that will breed and invite the next success. Once we come to recognize and believe the real power we have, we will be more willing to try again.

I remember many years ago being at a family get-together and enjoying a lovely conversation, when all of a sudden someone made a comment that felt like a put-down to me. I took the comment personally and confronted the relative for an apology after the get-together. Well, you guessed it, this pretty much started your basic family feud, with people choosing sides based on their interpretation of what took place. Feelings were hurt and the negative fallout left an awkward open wound. The relative lived out of state, so several months went by as the gap widened. At the time, the two of us were pregnant, with due dates very close to each other. Sound familiar? You know this kind of stuff happens every day in families and at work. We take offense at something and feel helpless. Sometimes we're on the receiving end and sometimes we're on the delivering end.

Now, here's where the rise above part comes in. As time drew nearer to our delivery dates, it occurred to me that the longer I let this go on the more difficult it would be to put behind us. I felt a certain responsibility for making it right again, even though I felt justified in my position at the time. But, *how* could I do it? It didn't seem easy. As a matter of fact, it felt risky and awkward. The only thing I knew was that my intention to help make it right was honest and sincere. I cared about this family. I realized that 20 years down the road if we had to explain why the family was fractured, it'd sound pretty ridiculous to our kids. I could just hear a 20-year-old saying, "Is that it? That's why I don't know my cousins?"

It took me a while to figure out the right approach. I definitely knew that calling and saying, "Look I was right and you were wrong, but..." wouldn't work. The real question was how I could leave both of us with some dignity without trying to determine a winner or loser and, more importantly, move on in a positive direction and put this *bump in the road* behind us. Once I decided to make that phone call, I fully knew the risks. So, I finally decided on the following approach. "You know this phone call isn't about who was right or who was wrong, it's about putting this behind us for the sake of our children and making things right. Life's too short." My real lesson came when the relative responded, "I'm so glad you called."

It was at that point that I realized the real lesson in *rising above*. Being rebuked is a possibility we can't let stand in the way of the healing process. Rising to a higher level of human functioning doesn't come naturally or easily because we're dealing with so much emotion and negative memory. Finding the *high ground common to both* probably holds the key. Find what you both have in common that could reunite. In this example, it was the awkwardness we both felt over something that shouldn't have happened.

To this day, 30 years later, the relationship I've just described has been wonderful. I would be terribly saddened and disappointed in myself had I left a gaping hole. You see, the longer we travel away from a negative incident two things happen over time: the gap widens while the issue diminishes in importance. It can become forgotten, silly, and insignificant.

I use this personal experience not because I think it's unique, but rather because it's not unique. Good people become trapped in *stupid, silly things* all the time and can't seem to find a good way out. It takes a real courageous person to find the key for getting past the challenge. Making things right whether we started them or not should always be our goal. Otherwise, the price we pay may be higher than the pain of the original dispute. Negative ripples are too far reaching for us not to look for that opportunity to *rise above*.

Of course, not every issue can be solved, but many issues can be if we try. Learning to rise above with integrity is an art. It's the gift of closure you give yourself and someone else you care about. I learned a valuable lesson through this challenge and it has offered me hope ever since. When good intention becomes apparent, people would much rather let go of the pain.

LESSON #71

STOP RUNNING THE RACE

I got this example from a television program several years ago that featured actor Dick Gregory who was helping honor comedian Richard Pryor. During the segment, Dick Gregory was recounting the tremendous challenges for black actors, singers, and comedians in the '50s. As he explained how they coped with discrimination despite their successes, he said one of the strategies they used was that they "stopped running the race and started running the relay." They created strength in numbers to build awareness for needed change. It's such a fundamental way to make improvements. Yet, so many of us just go it alone, thinking that we're the only one with a particular challenge. Support groups everywhere have created the relay for information to the masses. We need to stop suffering alone and stop accepting status quo. We need to recognize our own needs and rights and develop our network for reaching out.

Some wonderful examples recently have been in the area of breast cancer. Women are banding together in the fight for a cure by sponsoring fund-raising walks for research. Elizabeth Taylor was among the first to raise funds for AIDS research, at a time when many people had a "not my problem" attitude. Christopher Reeve is running the relay from his wheelchair and making his voice heard to advance a cure for spinal injuries. Michael J. Fox has used his diagnosis of Parkinson's disease to raise awareness and money. President and Mrs. Reagan have run the relay for Alzheimer's disease. Each of these causes began with one voice connecting with another voice in an attempt to make life better and eradicate these challenges. Katie Couric has run the relay for colon cancer awareness. Visibility and awareness are increased in numbers.

So often people can feel alone with a problem or unhappiness. More often than not, they're not alone. When we begin to reach out, we discover the relay to improve a less than wonderful predicament. This lesson is about recognizing our own rights to a better existence, as well as our right to be heard and advance the action. It happens one unlikely person at a time.

Whenever I deliver seminars or speak to groups, I often hear people comment on how relieved they are that they are not alone in their thinking or circumstances. Obviously, they felt alone or maybe were embarrassed because they hadn't successfully dealt with something. No question in my mind that there's a tremendous sense of relief once we realize that what we feel or think has happened to others. That awareness is the key to reaching out. Keeping things in and telling ourselves that *that's the way it is* can cause needless suffering.

It really points out the importance of developing *interdependence* with each other. Too much independence can hurt us because we will struggle alone. Telling ourselves that it doesn't matter anyway and no one is going to care are self-defeating. Support groups all over this country have brought voices and solutions to the many challenges people face. Reaching out and finding strength in numbers is a tremendous first step to improving our world. Jim Kelley, the former Buffalo Bills quarterback, and his wife Jill created Hunter's Hope for their son, Hunter, who was born a few years ago with fatal Krabbes disease. Their effort strengthens the ranks for research and a cure. Jumping into the forefront despite heartache wasn't easy, but their winning spirit emerged to begin making a difference. Our ability to make a difference is a testimonial to the greatness of people.

LESSON #72

IF YOU DON'T SET BOUNDARIES,
YOU SET YOURSELF UP

This lesson is for the used and abused. Okay, I guess we can all fall into that category at one time or another. The objective here is to reflect on whether we get used and abused due to our own inability to clearly state our expectations or request changes from others. The goal is to reduce disappointment and increase our ability to get more of what we need more of the time.

Very often passivity can get in the way of our wishes and dreams. I suppose we could take the position that it'll happen if it's meant to be. Or, we can clearly state our preferences and make requests to meet our needs. Now, the key to this lesson is to develop our ability to speak up assertively _before_ we get ticked off.

Let's say that you need to get the garage cleaned up for spring. You've got kids who could help out, who may not be adept at organizing or would easily be overwhelmed doing such a project. It's one of those family topics that when raised could easily be met with whining or resistance.

One approach might be to do it yourself, get no help, grumble, get frustrated, and resent those who didn't offer to pitch in on their own. And, _you_ become the proverbial martyr one more time.

Another approach might be to state your case diplomatically several days before the intended target date, lay out the different parts of the task, and offer everyone options and time frames as to when it could be accomplished. You could say, "Hey, guys, I'd like to get the garage cleaned out this weekend. I think it'll take a couple of hours with all four of us. So let's talk about time frames like Saturday morning or Sunday afternoon. I'm flexible. But let's pin it down tomorrow night so that all of us can enjoy the weekend and get the garage cleaned. I've got it broken down into four parts and we can each take one."

Obviously, the second approach clearly and diplomatically lays out a plan that enlists the help of others. Does that mean we always get what we want? No, but it does mean that we identify in our own minds *in advance* what boundaries we set and how others will assist in the effort. The alternative is to become a victim and have others depend on us for everything. This is about delegating and empowering those we care about because *they deserve the opportunity to learn.*

When my children were growing up, I remember that when I would do the wash, I couldn't help but notice how many pants my son wore since the last wash. My daughter, on the other hand, would have to wash that one blouse she absolutely needed for the next school day. I jumped on those opportunities to set new boundaries for them. If my daughter wanted that one blouse washed, she needed to check her other dirty clothes for all *like colors* before starting the washing machine. She was about 14 at the time. I also taught my son to do his own wash at 12 years old to help him understand the value of clean clothes. Interesting enough, I met no resistance at all. The timing seemed to work out well. They felt grown up and liked doing for it themselves.

What I did was take advantage of changes in their growing years to empower and teach them to look after themselves. A few years later, when my son went to college, he mentioned that when he went to the laundromat to do his wash, frequently women would compliment him on how well he did his wash and folding. Naturally, every time he told me, he would be smiling and quite proud of himself. He also noticed how many people during that freshman year had absolutely no idea how to take care of themselves. He quickly recognized how his training and skill made his transition much easier than many of his peers.

I've noticed over the years how easy it is for us to do for others and not realize that at some point there needs to be *new boundaries* and *new up-to-date expectations* for those little people we raise. We adults can too easily take the position, "I can do it faster and better anyway." Then the responsibilities keep piling up on us. People can become too dependent on others and expect we'll always do it. Think about the woman who has never written a check because her husband did it for 48 years before departing for the pearly gates. We may overlook the fact that our actions and lack of expectations develop deep-rooted dependency, fear of failure, and lack of self-confidence in others.

This lesson is really about looking for natural opportunities to transition, upgrade, and enlist the assistance of those around us. It's about taking seriously our responsibility to delegate to others to help them grow. It's teaching little children to start picking up their toys 30 minutes before lunch or dinner. It's building a team of people who work together rather than having one person do it all. It's more than learning to say no. It's helping others gain experience and skill.

In life, we don't automatically get what we deserve. We usually get part of what we negotiate and nothing if we don't negotiate. Speaking up assertively, recognizing our own rights, believing in possibilities, and influencing others will all help set the boundaries that can prevent us from being used and abused by others over time. If any particular situation comes to mind, then use this lesson. Come up with a plan and give it your best shot. Set that boundary, deliver the idea and expectation, and just maybe magic will happen!

LESSON #73

STOP STIRRING UP THE MUCK

Picture this. You've got a tall, fresh, clear glass of water. At the bottom happens to be a quarter inch of muck. If we picture *life* as that clear glass of water then we've got two choices. We can look at how much clear fresh water has accumulated in the glass or we can take out a spoon, put it in the glass, and stir up the muck. We can take what looks reasonably good and make it look just awful.

Some people are pretty good at stirring up the muck. I've often wondered why it is that people stir up the muck. It's about realizing when we've overdeveloped our focus on the negative and underdeveloped our ability to let go or move on. My guess is that people are not fully aware that their perspective has shifted so dramatically to the negative. I'm convinced that wonderful and good people can reach a point where their conversation is 90% negative, complaining, or rehashing. Just because they tell it in a humorous way doesn't make it any more positive.

I guess it plays into the misery *demands* company cliché. This lesson really goes to the heart of personal awareness about what *vehicle* we drive through life. Not only do we have a responsibility to be positive to live healthier, longer, but we have a responsibility as human beings to build each other up rather than taking each other down. Our focus should be on what goes well rather than what's disappointing. Disappointment happens to good people who deserve better. No one is exempt from that. *Life isn't always fair,* but how come we tend to notice the unfairness and fail to notice the blessings? In dealing with our feelings, though, we must keep ourselves from falling into this trap over and over again.

I remember one friend I grew up with who, like me, lived with personal challenges. After marrying a wonderful guy and moving on, she managed to carry along the burden of the past *long after* the issues were over. This approach contributed to harming the very people in her family who shouldn't have been harmed. This was a time of celebration and joy that became "mucky" unnecessarily. Learning to cope successfully can be accomplished by replacing negatives with successes, joys, or positives and focusing on how many positives we can stack on top of the negatives (just like that tall, fresh, clear glass of water). Time begins to heal the further away we get from the difficulty. A successful transition can be made easier by building successes one at a time to help put as much *good distance* as possible between the present and the negative history.

One coping strategy I've always liked is this one. You can put up with anything for a short time. This helps us *bite the bullet* during those challenging times and focus on moving forward once it's over. The goal is to stop stirring the muck so we can successfully leave it behind and move on to brighter times ahead.

LESSON #74

THE WISDOM OF AGE SHOULD NOT STIFLE THE ENERGY OF YOUTH

One thing I've learned about caring for someone is how easy it is to *prescribe* from our own autobiography. Knowledge, wisdom, and input are certainly valuable, but sometimes caring *too much* can play a part in preventing others from developing their own style. What comes to mind is the familiar college ultimatum, "As long as I'm paying for your college, here's what you're going to do." Or, here's another familiar one, "As long as I pay the bills, you'll do as I say." Remember this one? "As long as you live under my roof..."

I wonder if we really take stock in what the *generation gap* can really mean between people who care about each other. A few years ago, when my daughter was in her mid 20s, she was wondering why on earth boys wore such baggy pants drooping down so far. I told her it was the generation gap in motion! I guess every generation has its own unique *thing,* but one thing for sure is it'll always look strange to past generations who had a "better" *thing.* History is kind in that way, but I'm not sure we grow up with a proper perspective of what's relatively harmless generation to generation.

What we need to realize and factor in is that individuals need their life *customized and tailored* to fit them. So here's where the flexibility and adaptability come together, to create a winning combination between the wisdom of age and the energy of youth. Perhaps, as we reflect on personal disappointments or missed opportunities, we don't always realize how hardened we have become to closing doors on others. Another critical piece to factor in is that wisdom can never replace experience. One thing for sure is that experience learned the hard way is usually a lesson that will never be unlearned. We all learn from tough lessons.

As we get older and wiser, maybe we stop taking risks and discovering the spontaneity of our former youth. Especially if current thinking changes from our *known*, we may be less willing to entertain new possibilities. Youth wants it all as it should, and we need to be careful that we don't *rain on their parade*. For example, having never grown up with a cell phone or beeper, it would be difficult for me to actually pay for a 14-year-old to own a cell phone or beeper today. In many cases, we older and wiser folks have to understand and learn to deal better with the changing times. How many of us have rattled off the "I walked to school 5 miles in the snow with no boots" as a preface to blowing off a request from a child.

It occurs to me that people learn by experiencing and balancing the information they receive with their perception of how it plays out to help them reach their goals. We'd all have to admit that we are willing to put up with certain inconveniences if we want something badly enough. We need to remember that when coaching others to make decisions for themselves. The best way to influence someone else's behavior with personal wisdom is to be sure we understand clearly where the other person is coming from, how important it is to them, and what price they're willing to pay to make something happen.

One example comes to mind of something I personally dealt with. When I was growing up, no one lived together before marriage. Today, whether I like it or not and agree with it or not, this has changed. So, when my son was about to graduate from college, he ran the idea by me of moving in with his college girlfriend of one year. I knew it would be difficult to leave his friends and start over back home, but that didn't diminish my shock while he was calmly posing the question. Quickly I recognized my opportunity to influence rather than antagonize. The first thing I did was to keep my cool (while I'm dying and trying to gather some logical thoughts). I realize there is no training class when you're caught off guard, so hopefully my approach can help others identify a successful approach for them.

I began by explaining to my son that moving in with someone is a big step because without a marriage, it's never quite clear whose apartment it really is or to what extent the commitment exists (usually different for each). Who asks whom to leave? That doesn't sound like a fun thing to me. Breaking up is always hard without the additional pressure of territorial issues. Then I ran a scenario by him. What if he worked for a company with 250 of the best looking women he had ever seen? What if he started to be attracted to someone at work? How exactly would he explore the field as a single person? How exactly would he keep the door open to finding the right person? Then the scenario can really become ugly if someone resorts to sneaking around. All sense of value has now come into question and is being tested. After delivering my thoughts, I decided to turn the conversation over to my son. So, I said, "Well, Joel, you asked my opinion and now I'd like your opinion." His response blew me over. He said, "Well, Mom, you've kind of changed my mind." Whew! Whew! Whew! Once again I'm attempting to hide my real feelings of "yippee, hurray, my kid's coming home and I pulled it off."

What I learned is that sometimes it feels like you're walking a tightrope between what your head tells you and what today's youth face. Being accepting of changing times and balancing our wisdom with current thinking are things we really have to work on to be sure we're not delivering *out-*

dated advice to the new generation.

When I was 19 years old, I had already been working and making my own money when I decided to try wearing contact lenses. At that time, contacts were still very new and innovative (around 1966). The cost was about $200 but patients were able to try them for 30 days for $25. I had worn glasses since I was eight years old and hated wearing glasses. I still lived at home when I announced that I wanted to try contact lenses and would pay for them myself. Needless to say, I met a great deal of resistance including, "Mrs. So and So has them and she blinks like crazy all the time." While I was curious about the remark, it didn't stop me from proceeding. Then I was perceived as just plain stubborn and wanting to throw money away. Being true to myself and my youth was difficult, but I did it. Anyway, I adjusted beautifully to the contact lenses, had no problems, and went on to wear them for 33 years until getting Lasik eye surgery in 1999, which got rid of the contacts for good. Oh, happy day!

I certainly understand that the negative input comes from caring for someone too much. We need to allow people room to pursue what is truly important to them, respect their needs and dreams, and support their efforts even when they don't take our advice. Helping others examine their motives, shedding light on how to better deal with potential obstacles, and offering options to recover are really the best approaches if we care enough to help someone *learn* healthy decision making and healthy problem solving.

Our goal should be to channel youthful energy so that it builds the future. While we all lived in the good old days, *these are the good old days* for today's young people.

LESSON #75

THE GUILT TRIP

I'll admit it. I'm a work in progress when it comes to guilt. This lesson can help us strive to better deal with this human emotion. We can feel guilty over just about anything. *We shoulda, we coulda, we didn't know*, or any other guilt-inducing statement we run through our minds at a time of disappointment or confusion. We learn to feel guilty early. We can feel guilty on our own or others can make us feel guilty.

Growing up Catholic in the '50s, I remember learning at school with the good nuns that saying three Hail Marys before sleep every night would assure something, but I can't remember exactly what! I'd lie in bed starting to say them and realize I forgot which number I was on. So, I'd say another. I probably recited 10 Hail Marys making sure I was *under the wire*. A lot was at stake for an impressionable kid.

Questions like "*Why* did you do that?" "You ate *how much* dessert?" "Did I *say* you could do that?" "*How much* did you pay for that?" "You got *another* pair of shoes?" and "What do you need *that* for?" are statements by others that put us on the spot and make us feel guilty. Questions like these have us second guessing our own intentions and create guilt. People are very sensitive and take statements like these personally. Responding is difficult because it's an uphill battle to win the other person over. They obviously already think what you've done is ridiculous. Matters become worse if this situation occurs in a group of people. Guilt feelings are triggered when someone puts us on the spot. Their lack of sensitivity for another's feelings is evident.

For example, I enjoy dessert when eating out. Typically, people who don't eat dessert will kid me about getting *my dessert*. Honestly, I feel put on the spot and start feeling guilty over something I enjoy. I dread it when out with others. I've always told my husband that I don't understand why people do that. I'm not counting their drinks, so why are they counting my dessert? Why single someone out who is the only one interested in looking over the dessert menu? It would never occur to me to question why someone is ordering drinks. I don't drink, but I imagine a drink is to them what dessert is to me. It's an enjoyable part of the dining out experience. So if someone doesn't count your drinks, then stop counting their chocolate chip cookies! I can't even eat a hot fudge sundae or a banana split in peace these days, except with my family because we're all dessert eaters. Yummy!

Here's another one I'm sure many of you can relate to. Anybody else besides me have the habit of buying shoes frequently? I happen to like the right shoe with the right outfit. Here's a potential problem between spouses. The husband may say, "You bought another pair of shoes? For what? You don't have enough?" So let me clarify. Shoes are to women what gadgets at Sears are to men. It's easy to know if you make the other person feel guilty because moods change quickly and resentment builds. The other person begins mentally counting everything you do that they think is needless. Simply put, why should we resent what makes someone else happy? Use your humor. Support it rather than building another of life's sticking points upon which you'll probably get stuck! This is a no win situation! This world be a happier place if we communicated with more sensitivity and fewer guilt-laden statements. Let's support and show interest in each other's likes, dislikes, and decisions. Let's think before we speak and put a positive spin on what we say. It'll feel better and bring out the best in people!

LESSON #76

ARE YOU RESPONSIBLE FOR OR
ARE YOU RESPONSIBLE TO?

Years ago my friend, Ilene Baker, shared a wonderful phrase with me that proved to be an interesting lesson which I will share with you. It's a great question to pose to yourself. "Who are you responsible *for* and who are you responsible *to?*" It's a fine distinction to help us better deal with what we can control versus what we can't completely control.

You can only be responsible *for yourself* and you can only be responsible *to others.* Understanding what is within our power will better help us deal with limitations while putting our best foot forward. One example might be if a child does something negative, like drinking too much or getting arrested. Too often we start questioning ourselves as to what we could have done to prevent it. The embarrassment can feel like a reflection of us personally or our parenting skills. We often agonize over what other people will think or how we will explain it to or face others. Most of us have heard "your friends will understand but your enemies won't."

In this case, we are *responsible to* our children by educating them, giving them values, and being vigilant by providing proper supervision. However, we cannot be responsible for every thought and every behavior their free will allows. Kids learn to sneak around early on if they want to do something they know is not acceptable.

We are also *responsible to* others around us in the world we live in and the people we interact with day-to-day. A tiny example that comes to mind is when you're using the ladies room and happen to notice too late that there is no toilet paper left. Don't you wonder what on earth the last person was thinking as she ripped off the last few sheets? You hate to think it was, "I'm glad *I* had enough." Are people so shortsighted that they fail to see their *responsibility to* use the information they possess to benefit others? It doesn't take a rocket scientist to figure out that a problem has been identified. It's everyone's responsibility to share information to achieve better outcomes and prevent unnecessary problems. Another silly example is when we finish using something, like eating the last slice of cheese. Our responsibility is to jot it down on a grocery list for the person who buys groceries.

First, we can only be *responsible for* ourselves and our behavior. Second, we can be *responsible to* others for sharing the best of what we know while accepting the limitations of our influence.

LESSON #77

MAKE SURE YOU HAVE A TRIPTIK

How many of you have ever gotten a Triptik from AAA when traveling somewhere? Well, when we drive somewhere typically my husband drives and I have the Triptik. Triptiks keep me busy instead of asking "are we there yet?" a hundred times. I get to check out which cities we pass through, where the next stop might be, and any other details available in the Triptik. My question for you is who has the *power* in our car, the person driving or the person with the Triptik? Some may say the driver because the driver controls the steering wheel to get there. Some may say the navigator because the navigator controls the directions. Some may say both the driver and the navigator because one can't get there without the other. The answer is both.

What I want to illustrate with this example is the power everyone can have if they choose to. In life, there'll be a driver, there'll be a navigator, and there'll be someone along for the ride. This example helps identify what position you take as you *drive through life*. Maybe you're happy with the *going along for the ride* as you're *driving through life*. Maybe you're happy as the *navigator* or maybe as the *driver*. This lesson is about being conscious of the decisions you make personally or professionally on a day-to-day basis.

Sometimes, people find themselves with a *driver* and decide to go along for the ride. In that case, you settle for whatever the *driver* wants. By offering no input, you accept whatever happens. In this position, the person going along for the ride really has no business complaining. When you don't contribute or participate, you accept whatever happens.

Sometimes you find yourself with a *driver* and decide to be a *navigator*. This example can illustrate those challenges that you may find yourself facing at home or at work. They are issues that have been put on you by your surroundings or environment. When you feel controlled by a *driver*, it becomes your job to get a *Triptik* and then begin navigating to figure out where you let this lead. In this example, you reclaim personal power even though you feel powered by some other driver. You take a *leading role* as a *navigator* rather than just going *along for the ride*.

This lesson is about regaining personal power when feeling that circumstances are beyond your control. It is critical that we realize the choices we have. We can *let life happen* or we can *lead life to happen* by stacking the odds in our favor. The world may tell you with its thinking of the day that something is not possible. People defy *thinking of the day* all the time because some unique piece of discovery is just enough to improve the outcome. Sometimes we take the *thinking of the day* too literally. One thing you can count on is that the *thinking of the day* has exceptions. Those in a leadership role will discover them. Those along for the ride will not.

LESSON #78

THE GREAT ESCAPE

I love picturing things in my mind as a way to help me relate to them. One thing that seems amazing to me is how Houdini, the great escape artist, spent his life creating problems to solve with the whole world watching. Most of us would prefer solving problems privately, that's for sure. You know, in case you fail. Why expose weaknesses to the world?

Houdini represents the power of persistence and possibility by developing determination, commitment, problem solving, and closure by never giving up. Frankly, these habits are nice alternatives to panic, worry, frustration, and unsolved mysteries. Don't you hate living with something you never figure out and you sort of agonize over the why? You could say that Houdini taught us that *conquering problems and fear* can be very personally rewarding. It's so easy to say, "No, not me, not today," as we take the easiest way out. His example illustrates the courage any of us can muster to face head on whatever challenge life deals us.

Winners who successfully *escape* the ravages of personal or professional challenge are born every day. I think of my dear friends Fran and Rosanne, whose second child was born with life threatening problems. He required tube feeding and had a poor prognosis. They almost lost him several times. Life expectancy was very short. Today their child is approaching 20 years old. They've kept him at home, loved him, and given him a superior quality of life, while successfully managing their own quality of life. They are truly a couple of life's *Houdinis*. In addition to dealing successfully with this child, they went on to adopt three children. They annually sponsor a large fundraiser to raise money for the school their son attends. Escaping with success that seems nothing short of magic is what this couple accomplished. They are an inspiration.

Another couple of friends, Susan and Bob, have also inspired me with their *magic*. Susan and Bob had a lovely baby daughter after two sons. Six months after her birth, their lovely new baby developed seizures and they were thrust into the abyss of medical uncertainty. They were told their child possibly might never potty train. There were more questions than answers. They faced a bleak outlook from a medical standpoint. Then, they went to work to become *Houdinis* on behalf of their daughter. She did potty train due to Susan's relentless belief in possibility and the parents' focus on improving the quality of her life. She's also been successfully mainstreamed into the classroom as a result of their pursuit for as normal a life as they can possibly provide for her. Their daughter is a very happy and lovely young person. They truly worked magic with the hand they were dealt.

These are just a couple of outstanding real life and real people examples of regaining personal power in the face of incredible personal challenge. The good news is that there are *magicians* like them everywhere who display the tremendous characteristics of courage and persistence when faced with unknown and impossible odds.

This book is a tribute to people who become life's magicians and literally create magic before the world's eyes. They're not the rich and famous. Their stories have never appeared on *Dateline*. Maybe you're thinking, "I'm a magician" because you have a story like these. The world may not highlight your personal story, but you should always feel good about the personal power you put forth to create life's magic. To regain your personal power at every turn, think about

Houdini and how you too can survive against the odds for a successful escape. When you first picture the potential for escape, you actually begin the magic.

LESSON #79

FORGIVENESS IS...

While we all have developed a perception of what forgiveness means to us, it's very easy to talk ourselves out of forgiving anyone for anything. Keeping hard feelings is probably pretty easy to do. Depending upon how deep the hurt goes or what sensitive issue was affected, forgiveness can be tough. Typically, we find ourselves saying, "Well, I can forgive but I can't forget" or, "I can't forgive because I can't forget."

This lesson is about the real mental leap and the high road to freedom. Have you ever heard the phrase *"whatever angers you controls you?"* It's what begins to eat away at our stomachs. It's when our thoughts are overtaken with pain and anguish. It's when we've become hostages to someone or something outside ourselves. It's a heart wrenching challenge. We may frequently find ourselves dealing with the issue of forgiveness. The goal is to achieve a positive rather than painful outcome.

One day, while watching an episode of Oprah Winfrey, I happened to catch a segment in which she was talking about forgiveness. I'm the type of person who retains better with a story or short catchy phrase. Anyway, Oprah's definition of *forgiveness* made it a lot clearer to me. She explained that forgiveness is not about *approving* what someone else did. It rather is about *accepting* that it happened in order to facilitate healing. It's about accepting that unfortunate occurrences happen to everyone. At the same time, wonderful things happen, too. It's very easy for people to read way too much into the unfortunate. It's an easy way to begin feeling like a victim rather than achieving a victor approach.

We all need to develop our ability to let go and move on. Time can heal by putting distance between the *unforgivable* and allow us one day to forgive. We need to talk to ourselves to resolve the issue internally so that we can move away from anger and revenge. Think of all the stories about those who find a way to forgive murderers. Most of us would say "impossible!" I heard a story about a young reporter named Laura who went undercover to get to know the man accused of attempting to murder her father in a foreign country. She made it her goal to have the accused know how wonderful the man was that he attempted to kill. What she discovered was incredible. She discovered his sorrow, and began a friendship with his family. She successfully closed a circle most of us would never attempt to close.

We can get to a better place when we accept that unfortunate things will happen to good people. People may not like us because of their perception of who we are. Perhaps we didn't have as much in our childhood as we would have liked. Perhaps we've missed job opportunities we should have gotten. Forgiveness will cut us loose from agony when we accept our own frailty and the frailty of others. Forgiveness is not about approval, but rather about acceptance that can help us let go and move on to assure that we are not *lost as a victim,* due to someone else's frailty.

LESSON #80

SEPARATE WHO YOU ARE
FROM WHAT HAPPENS TO YOU

This lesson reflects our ability to keep our heads above water if we're drowning in a sea of adversity. It's about the success stories of those who beat the odds against incredible challenge to create their own unique masterpiece of success. Whatever garbage gets thrown *at* us, we can never *become* garbage. Years ago I remember hearing, "God doesn't make junk." I can't say I completely understood the depth of that phrase then. My understanding has deepened over the years through personal experience and observing the heroics of others.

It's so easy to get sucked into an *eye for an eye* approach. It's the old *I hit him because he hit me* scenario. Staying focused and not allowing outside distractions to derail our hopes and dreams is not easy. While my first 20 years of life were difficult, somehow I was able to *separate who I was and my dreams for a better life.* In Viktor Frankl's book *The Meaning of Life*, he writes about the second way to deal with difficulty which is to *picture life after the difficulty.* It's the technique he used as a prisoner of war. It's a very powerful coping strategy that allows us to mentally remove ourselves from the negative circumstances and picture ourselves in a place we want to be. It's creating hope where there is none. It begins within our own minds. Behavior follows how we talk to ourselves.

Many people have displayed this marvelous ability while it seems to elude others. The success of so many African-Americans against the odds serve as a shining example of how they separated who they were from what happened to them. Peoples and nations face this all the time. There is a wonderful movie called *Men of Honor*. It stars Robert DeNiro and Cuba Gooding, Jr. It is the real life story of Navy diver Carl Brashear during World War II. It portrays his difficult pursuit to become the first African-American accepted into the Navy's diving program. He was finally accepted only after writing hundreds of letters. The story goes on to show how Carl successfully continued to deal with resistance throughout his Navy career. Ultimately, he received the highest honor the Navy bestowed on divers.

Stories like that help us realize what it sometimes takes to achieve the success that eludes us. His incredible ability to continue the fight to separate *who he knew he was* from what seemed to be his plight helps all of us put our own challenges in perspective. Obstacles can be removed one by one when we want something badly enough and we picture ourselves in the place we want to be. The mind is very powerful. Our success begins with picturing the possibility, then building a reality around that picture while successfully navigating obstacles. Carl Brashear dealt successfully with disappointment all his life. His example is a great lesson for us all!

LESSON #81

IF YOU THINK
GETTING RICH IS TOUGH

If you think getting rich is tough, then try making ends meet! No one ever said becoming financially comfortable was easy. What I have difficulty with is the rationale from those who are not financially comfortable. They may rationalize their position as one that's desirable because they get by and prefer the simple life.

It's a bit scary to me when people forget to *pass on possibility* to the next generation. Frankly, I don't ever remember anyone, including those in the educational system, coaching us to be whatever we wanted to be. I don't remember anyone showing us the way or helping us open doors. Frankly, I don't remember anyone impressing on us the importance of education to open our own doors. I thought maybe it was just the '50s and '60s, but I've discovered that many people who were not wealthy during those years somehow managed to find their way to college.

It's made me realize that we need to teach people how to go for the gold ring. It's up to them to decide whatever they choose to achieve. Perhaps times have changed but I believe we have the responsibility as adults to coach our young people to have it all. They should at least have an opportunity to weigh in on how much of *it all* they're willing to work for.

This lesson is not about copying the rich. It's about having the opportunity to be ourselves with all options on the table. People deserve to know how some achieve what they choose. People need to be supported in the pursuit of their dreams.

It's not uncommon for young people to dream about making $100,000 a year and driving a Porsche. They don't need some adult ridiculing their dream by saying, "Yeah, right" or, "I'm *still* waiting." My question is when did *we* stop being kids? When did we decide dreams are hopeless? When did we decide that making ends meet would do? When exactly did we give up? Why do we negatively influence others to stay put?

I often wonder if sometimes we unconsciously rain on another's parade to safeguard ourselves by assuring that they stay where *we are*. Is it a way of validating and securing our own position? Perhaps, if others figure out how to "make it" we might have to seriously consider why they *did* and we *didn't*.

Picture someone trying to touch their fingertips in front of them and then just when they are about to meet, some stronger force pulls them apart again. Every attempt at having their fingertips meet results in the same resistance and struggle. That's how I describe having *ends meet*. You never quite get there. You're always slightly off the mark but always hoping the results will be different. Struggling is painful. To me it's like adjusting to a limp because it never feels right. Do we even realize that struggling can be of our own making?

On the other hand, while life offers no guarantees, moving forward and advancing the action hold the only true hope of making a better life for ourselves and our children. Is it easy? No. I can think of several foreign doctors who've come to the United States and had to start all over. One particular friend of ours had been a long-time internist in another country. When he had to start over in this country, the only residency program available to him was in Psychiatry, so he became a psychiatrist. He would have done whatever it took to begin anew. No matter how long it took, he was committed to making his dream a reality.

The one place in our life for *adaptive struggling* should be the struggle and sacrifice of getting ahead to a non-struggling future. Pioneers and immigrants built this country. People left their homelands to start over with nothing. Everyone needs to learn to struggle. We all face it at some time in our lives. But we should not automatically accept struggle as a permanent existence. Turning struggle around is always a possibility. Our job becomes finding opportunities. Too many are afraid to risk leaving their comfort zone or are unwilling to make the sacrifices it takes for their future.

This lesson comes from the heart from a person who knows the reality and difficulty of *securing* her own future. Successful people picture possibilities, formulate plans for making them happen, and have been coached and supported to make them happen. Life is difficult enough without stifling the God-given potential, talent, and uniqueness of any human being. Everyone has the power to achieve. Let no caring adult laugh at or stand between any person and the dream to reach for the stars. As a matter of fact, if you get there before me, reach down and help me up!

LESSON #82

EXCUSES, EXCUSES, EXCUSES

Have you ever noticed that winners don't make excuses? The reason they don't make excuses is because they're too busy making it happen, and assuring that they have it all. The better a person gets at developing winner thinking, the less the person makes excuses.

There are people who are the *excuse kings* and *queens* of the world. They've always got an excuse for everything. As a matter of fact, their excuses get quite sophisticated, detailed, and unbelievable. That's the key. They are unbelievable. The difference between a *reason* and an *excuse* is that an excuse often represents poor planning, lack of organization, lack of insight, or poor judgment. Usually the only person believing the excuse is the person delivering it. Everyone hearing it is wondering which of the above reasons was behind the excuse. A reason, on the other hand, is an obstacle that could not have been foreseen. *9/11 was a reason not to get somewhere because the airports were getting shut down.* Getting to work late because of morning traffic is an excuse. Every morning has traffic. We need to factor that in to arrive on time. Trying to just squeeze by is a key to excuses.

Excuses often accompany issues that are no surprise to us, but somehow we tell ourselves that a good excuse will defer the negative judgment by others. It doesn't. People who are consistently late for deadlines or appointments, no matter how many intelligent excuses they deliver, need to manage their time more effectively. Somehow they haven't figured out that they are ineffective time managers. They mistakenly think that their excuses make their behavior okay but they don't.

Making a lot of excuses is a key symptom of a deeper problem not being addressed. Those making excuses daily, either personally or professionally, have to stop unrealistically hoping the world will work perfectly for a change. They have to stop "banana-peel" living, that is, *sliding in just under the wire on a banana peel.*

Making excuses goes to the heart of personal performance standards. What do we expect of ourselves? What do others expect of us? Do we care enough to be accountable to those we serve or rub elbows with? This lesson is about taking a hard look at whether we use the *excuse crutch to limp through our existence* or whether we depend on awareness, knowledge, and skill to overcome the habit of making excuses by replacing them with action, solutions, and prevention. The good news is that personal dependability goes up dramatically when we replace excuses with winner thinking and winning ideas.

LESSON #83

EVERYONE HAS A MASTERPIECE

Remember doing those connect-the-dot pictures you did as a kid? We'd all try to figure out the picture without connecting the dots. We'd just try to figure it out by looking at it. Remember putting pencil to paper and quickly finding one number after the other while not quite sure where you were headed? Remember times when you couldn't locate the next number? While you struggled to find that *stupid* number, you'd talk yourself into the idea that the puzzle must have a mistake. Suddenly, out of the blue, you'd find it and wonder why you missed it. Then, as you took the not so obvious path, the picture began to form. Only after heading in a direction you couldn't figure out, you'd come to see what the author saw. Weren't you amazed you couldn't see it earlier? Seems so simple after the fact.

Our lives are like connect-the-dot masterpieces. No two are alike. That's why life can be so difficult. While we can get advice from others, who have progressed on their connect-the-dot masterpieces, we must balance their insight with what we see on ours. Wouldn't it be nice if someone else were to just map out our success for us? Truth is, there really is no substitute for thinking for yourself based on your needs and circumstances.

Information and knowledge from others can serve to enlighten us on broader issues, make us think of considerations we hadn't thought of, potentially eliminate unnecessary setbacks, or help us discover shortcuts. However, in the long run, we're on our own. Sometimes our masterpiece gets scary and we can feel like there's a big mistake. We can't see where the next dot connects and we panic. But, before long the picture forms and comes back into focus. These passages in our masterpiece are part of life leading us in directions we might not have chosen for ourselves. I can certainly attest to the fact that there was no time in my life I thought I'd become an author until I was faced with career changes that motivated me to start a speaking career. It was definitely a "dot" I didn't see coming.

This lesson is about faith in yourself, faith in your ability to thrive in a different situation, faith in possibility that runs into you, and faith in your ability to rebound from disappointment. Think of disappointment as those times when you cannot see the next dot. All of a sudden the picture you thought was there has changed. Always remember there's still a picture and it's your masterpiece. As long as you live, you can connect those dots and see a bigger picture emerging. Struggle can lead us to a better place when we have faith in ourselves. In the wake of your life, your masterpiece will be there for the world to see, appreciate, and learn from. I think I see your next dot right there. See it? Right there. Yeah, there it is!

SOMETIMES YOU KNOW WHERE IT'S GOING, SOMETIMES YOU DON'T!

LESSON #84

LIFE IS NOT LIKE A SLOT MACHINE

Ever been to a casino in Las Vegas, Reno, or Atlantic City? I'm always so amazed by the traffic and the number of gamblers at the nickel machines. It's amusing to see the *veteran gamblers* implementing their straregy. I always get a kick out of the old women at the nickel machines. Not only are they implementing their strategy, but this is serious business. Even looking like you're waiting for their machine can get you some pretty dirty looks. It's comical because we're talking about nickels for heaven's sake.

This example is an easy parallel to just how much or how little we put into our own personal advancement. Even if we win at the nickel machines, the winnings won't get us very far. A good story to tell and that's about it. Okay, so maybe we're just in it for the fun of it. Hopefully, with life, we're in it for a little more than just the fun of it, or putting in our time waiting for something better.

One reality we all need to face is *you can't get out what you don't put in.* If we just do what it takes to squeeze by then squeezing by is probably all we'll get. We do some things in life for the fun and we don't expect a return on investment. However, certainly our well-being and the well-being of our family critically depend on what sacrifices we're willing to make to achieve a secure future.

If you don't feel like you're paying a price, then you're probably not. If you're not in a situation that challenges you, then your growth will be limited. Life is really about checks and balances. We've got to be willing to extend then bal-

233

ance, extend then balance, and extend then balance some more. It's *so* easy to just settle for what we have. One day rolls into the next and our complaints revolve around the price of gas or the electric bill going up because our success *increase* doesn't keep up with inflation. There can come a time on the road of life when we're actually going backward and don't even realize it until we've got debt coming out our ears.

These can be hard lessons learned. The good news is that once we make the decision to *make life happen* instead of *letting life happen*, we can then invest what is appropriate to reach our goals. Achieving success will always be hard work and feel tough as we push ourselves out of our comfort zones. Opening new doors will always lead us away from the *nickel machines* and up to where better investments pay off long term. Stretching and growing, at any age, keep us viable and excited about life. I always kid around that if I was relatively successful by age 40, when I hardly had a clue about what was going on for 25 of those years, then imagine how successful I can be now that I've learned a lesson or two. The sky's the limit, so let's kick it up a notch and continue to raise our personal expectations for ourselves and our future.

LESSON #85

WHEN JUDGMENT DAY ARRIVES

When judgment day arrives, will you be charged with *loitering on earth?* Many of us can relate to a *day of reckoning,* when we have to account for our treasure chests and exactly what we accomplished with the life we were given. The challenge is that there is no dress rehearsal. Those who make excuses will be ready with their laundry lists of *unbelievable* obstacles, but they won't fool anyone but themselves. Many of us would admit that *life is too short,* which is all the more reason to give value to our time spent.

It's always sad to see retired people who seem to devalue life after they leave the workplace. It's like they see retirement as a finish line. A friend's mother died at about 82 and she had two jobs right up until she got sick. She was excited every day about being active and productive. Willa Mae, my housekeeper for 17 years, died unexpectedly at 76. She had cleaned for me just prior to going into the hospital. I would never have let her go because of her age. If I had, then she would have been wallpapering her living room or something like that. She had a young person's energy and excitement. I can think of another friend's mother, Jo, who at 92 years old, plays bridge weekly, drives, and entertains. She golfed until she was 90. No *loitering* for her. My hat is off to senior citizens who own computers, e-mail, surf the Internet, and stay right up to speed so they don't miss out on the technology revolution. No *loitering* for them. They keep reinventing themselves. They don't see a need to start winding down. Even though life may be short, they look at every day as another opportunity to advance. They don't want to miss anything. They're dying to live rather than living to die.

Dr. Leo Buscaglia, a speaker from California I heard years ago, told a story once about running into an old homeless man in the park. They began chatting and Dr. Buscaglia asked him if he had any regrets. The man said, "I'd eat more ice cream and less beans." I guess he would have enjoyed more and denied himself less. Maybe he thought his life lacked luster and he just began wasting it away, thinking it didn't matter much.

Loitering is about halting or slowing personal achievement. It's taking the path of least resistance. It's wasting our talent and potential rather than giving it value. It's one day rolling into the next with not much to show for it. We all know that *intelligence alone* does not guarantee success. We all know that *opportunity alone* is never enough to succeed. What can make a difference is our commitment and determination to be sure we don't waste the years away.

There are married people who say, "I don't *have to* work." Are they implying that successful partnering has exempted them from individual achievement? Personal achievement goes to the heart of positive self-esteem. Personal achievement is directly connected to a person's self worth. Where and when did we ever get the idea that someone else should be our meal ticket? There is a book called *Men Are Just Desserts*. The message from that book is that we first have to be secure in ourselves. Partners are like *good desserts* that add to something already fulfilling (ourselves). A partner's success does not automatically spill over to create personal success or happiness for us. It is not a replacement for personal growth and development.

So, when you get to the pearly gates to give an accounting of your treasure chest and how you spent your life and time, stand tall and say, "I wasn't loitering. No way. No siree. Here are my accomplishments…"

LESSON #86

THE LEARNING CURVE

One time my husband and I were discussing the learning curve and I asked him how I could illustrate it rather than just talk about it. It's one of those things that we all assume everyone understands. It wasn't until we talked about it that I gained a better understanding of what the learning curve means to us day-to-day. Many of us might feel funny actually asking someone to explain the learning curve because we understand the two words separately. In application, I'm not sure we've gotten the lesson intended based on what it means to us. On a day-to-day basis, the learning curve is about preparing for being frustrated the first time you do anything. The ninetieth time you do the task, you're on a roll. Frustration actually decreases along the way as you get better each time you perform the task. The task becomes second nature.

Think of all those people for years who couldn't program a VCR. I remember calling my son at college to have him walk me through it over the phone. He could picture any of our three VCRs. So, my learning usually began with the rhetorical question, "Mom, how many times have I taught you this?" Then I'd run through my excuses, "I hate it. It doesn't make sense. I don't do it often enough. So tell me one more time or I stop sending money." He would kill himself laughing at how I struggled through the simplest steps. *Truth is, it wasn't until I wrote down my own step-by-step directions that I was able to pull it off without him.* Now, I'd love to tell you I learned it after 2 or 3 times, but it was more like 40 or 50 times before I could accomplish the task without using my notes. When performing a task so discouraging that we give up, we need to find our own way to achieve a successful outcome.

No matter how old we get, we shouldn't *act* old. Fortunately for me, VCRs have gotten easier to master or just maybe I'm further along the learning curve. And, in this world of technology, I'm glad I am. These fast-paced times are leaving many behind. I recently bought a storage cabinet that required some assembly. Although assembling something myself is not my forte, I wanted to see if I could do it. I can't tell you how proud I was of myself after I assembled that cabinet without help.

I'm not sure we do people a favor when we don't allow them to progress on their own learning curve. Doing everything *for others* and not *showing them how* to do things can be a real disservice. It's so easy to do something ourselves because we can do it faster and better. However, all the while, we've got someone left behind that learning curve of life. It's exciting to figure something out that we've never done. Let's not rob others of the opportunity to learn new skills. I've often wished that my high school had offered *shop* because I still feel so inadequate with tools. I remember when my son took sewing in grammar school and made a wonderful stuffed camel. What a thrill! It was one less mystery and one less stumbling block for him. The learning curve can be frustrating with computers, for example, but it is *one way* to stay ahead in a fast changing world.

LESSON #87

TRAGEDY VERSUS OPPORTUNITY

While a chunk of this book is dedicated to avoiding *victim* mentality, that can become pretty hard to do if we're blindsided by *life* tossing in some tragedy that we didn't choose. Timing isn't particularly important either when life comes calling in some tragic, inopportune way. Over the years, it's occurred to me that we really have to beat *life* before it beats us. Too frequently, after dealing with some difficulty, we find ourselves just floundering and glad things are over. To regain positive momentum instead, we need to jump-start our turn around *when life's not looking.*

Taking advantage of opportunity is not something we ought to put off, because for whatever time we have some of that time will be eaten up by negative events. This lesson also goes to the heart of making our *good* time count and count well. Recent events in history have delivered one incredible wake-up call for all of us. Life has been put in perspective again by refreshing our memories about what's really important.

Living with regret over missing opportunity is in many cases needless. Trying to live without regret is well worth pursuing. None of us can be perfect. Hopefully, we can take the time to be sure we make time for opportunities, both personal and professional, that help us better cope with those difficult events put upon us.

Making a conscious choice is really a wonderful coping skill over that which is imposed. Seeing choice and opportunity are great ways to picture life after a difficult time, so that we

can move onward and upward with greater ease and put ourselves back on a winner's track to success. If your train gets
thrown off track, then get it back on track and work to regain
what you lost. It's that long list of things we want to do that
we can focus on as a way to get ourselves through challenge.
It'll provide that extra push to extricate ourselves from the
unpleasant. It'll provide the motivation to survive, move on,
and continue on the path to success.

LESSON #88

PEOPLE LEARN BY LOOKING AROUND

Can you think of how many times you've noticed someone who seems like they just couldn't care less? It's almost as if they are unaware of how indifferent they appear in the eyes of others. The environment we live in certainly affects what we come to learn as *normal*. Here are a couple of the many ways we learn. One way we learn is by being chastised for doing something we shouldn't be doing. Another way we learn is by looking around and observing what we see as normal behavior.

We all share the responsibility for being on the team as role models for others. Scrooge, in *A Christmas Story*, had become a very cynical "humbug" person. After seeing that story over and over, we almost tell ourselves that "Scrooges" really don't exist, but they do. Just like in the story, it can take someone's positive example to turn Scrooge back into the good person he had the potential to be. His nastiness was only a symptom.

Being a positive example for others is so important to the learning experience. One example that comes to my mind was a speaking program I did with a school system. They had a number of elective classes offered and my program was delivered in a classroom. As I entered the classroom, it was obvious that the teacher in the class made no attempt whatsoever to tidy up in preparation for this training. It occurred to me that the underlying visual message to students was probably a lot louder than any message they *heard* the teacher deliver. The underlying messages were that messes and disorganization can't be helped, are just part of doing your job, and taking responsibility for being organized isn't important.

Watching others successfully problem solve teaches us logic instead of panic or hopelessness. Watching others succeed teaches us how success can work for us. Watching others set goals, be positive, and show enthusiasm will give greater joy to existence. Watching others believe in possibility develops our sense of can-do. Learning from the success of others will help us to succeed. People learn by looking around and seeing the obvious and not so obvious. If we deal successfully with angry people, we teach others around us that this can be done successfully, without undue stress. When we treat others with courtesy and respect, we teach courtesy and respect. Soon others figure out there is a higher level of functioning. Duplicating the success becomes possible.

Great role models inspire others to learn what it takes to become better than the average. Winners help us set higher standards for personal expectation and performance. This lesson is about making sure that *we* are *winning role models* and that we are the best we can possibly be. Why? The answer is because it feels great, it is empowering, and it is what every person needs and deserves to take their best shot at *success in life*. It's what we want to pass on to our children and anyone we rub elbows with. What goes around, comes around.

LESSON #89

PUT SOME CHUNKIES IN SOMEONE'S LIFE

One of the greatest joys in life is honoring someone else. How many times have you heard people say, "I'll call you," and they never do. "We'll have to get together," and it never happens. This lesson is about becoming mindful of positive connections with people. Connecting with people is so easy. All we have to do is make sure we give it importance, so that our personal message to others supports the "I care about you" and "I want to be with you" messages.

Whether it's about getting together with family, friends, people at work, or neighbors, one thing that will never change is that everyone's busy. So, what else is new? Let's make a commitment to stop allowing life's excuses to erode the important feelings we have for those important to us.

Over the years of observing families with adult children, it's occurred to me that frequently the parents become the "go to" connections in the family. Brothers and sisters don't always take the time to nurture the sibling relationships separately from the parents. How fortunate we are to have family, yet sometimes we take advantage of that relationship by assuming it's just always going to be there. It comes back to the saying, "You can't get out what you don't put in." It's like the nickel slot machine. There's no million-dollar jackpot there. Ask yourself what you do to treat people special, whether they're parents, spouses, children, siblings, nieces or nephews, friends, neighbors, or strangers.

Connections come from doing special little things that become your unique tradition for others. I remember when I was 5 or 6, my Aunt Lucy and Uncle Frank had me over for dinner on Friday nights. There would always be a nickel under my dinner plate. If I live to be a hundred, I'll never forget that nickel under my dinner plate. It was a connection that carried a powerful message that said, "You're special."

I remember when my Dad came home from work, my brother and I ran up to the corner to meet him. We were still young and he'd bounce us up and down on his forearms before making us fish in his pockets for the Chunky he had hidden for each of us. At the time, he worked in a quarry and wore layered clothing that had lots of pockets to fish in. I still remember giggling like crazy, fishing for that Chunky. As difficult as life was back then, I can still hear my Mom saying, "Well, tonight's treat night." That usually meant getting ice cream.

Taking the time to call friends in the midst of our busy lives is a very important connection. Life's so short. Waiting for the other person to initiate the call because it's "their turn" is like taking a backseat on an important issue. Make the time to do special things.

Engaging others in conversation rather than doing all the talking is a wonderful way of honoring others. Asking for people's opinions and showing interest in them are easy ways to convey respect and caring. My husband, Steve, is the best at this particular skill. There's no question in my mind, I've learned it better as I observe him make people feel so valued within the framework of a conversation. My good friend, Helene, who was my inspiration to become a speaker, used to say, "When was the last time you spoke to the janitor?" How easy it is to discount others when we need each other so very much.

Recently I lost a very dear friend, Charlotte, at the young age of 64. She was the queen of thoughtfulness. In her last few weeks, I would remind her of all the wonderful things she had done for others all her life. She looked at me and said, "You do for others when you're needed." She said it so matter-of-factly. She was an absolute shining example of bringing out the best in others. If a friend were hospitalized, Charlotte would be the one who brought a complete homemade dinner over the day you came home. Her last days were spent with people who came out of the woodwork to honor her. She lived a life of honoring people. How could we do less for her in her time of need?

We have two choices. We can either make life happen or let life happen. Connections with people can't wait. They add so much value to our lives. Let us take the time to honor people and bring out their best. When we do, we bring out the best in ourselves!

LESSON #90

GET OUT OF YOUR OWN WAY

Some people in this world wait for things to happen. Some people in this world live in the state of denial hoping things will happen as they observe the odds stacked against them with time slipping away. Some people in this world wish they would just win the lottery to solve it all. Some people in this world spend their time assessing the fairness of it all and why they don't have what others have. Some people in this world distract themselves with some nasty habits.

Here's one of my favorite stories that illustrates our ability or inability to take responsibility for ourselves and our actions. There was a man named Sol who lived in a place where flooding was a problem. Whenever the water rose, he had the same routine. He would go to the roof and wait for the water to subside. Then he went back into his house after it was over. It always worked the same. One time, as the water rose, it became necessary to evacuate again. As the first lifeboat came to get Sol, he shouted from the rooftop, "My faith will not be shaken, God will save me." As the water continued to rise to the second floor, the second lifeboat came by and again Sol said, "My faith will not be shaken, God will save me." By now the water had reached the roof as the third lifeboat arrived. The rescuers pleaded with Sol to get in because it was his last chance. Again he said, "My faith will not be shaken, God will save me." Sol drowned and went to heaven. He met God and said, "I have one question. My faith was not shaken. Why didn't you save me?" God said, "Sol, I sent *three* lifeboats!"

We miss opportunity all the time and very often *miss the*

boat. Opportunity exists everywhere and every day if we would simply learn to recognize it, take advantage, and be willing to push ourselves. It's so easy to just repeat what's always gotten us by, without realizing that what used to work fine may stop working because our world or circumstances change. It's always easier to take the path of least resistance. This lesson is about becoming vigilant and mindful. It's about carefully assessing and monitoring our direction in case it's time to get into a lifeboat.

Assessing a situation quickly and accurately is a *skill* we can develop to assure that we don't waste our time or our lives, *standing in line waiting our turn,* as the parade passes by. Too often people just do what everyone else does, whether it's standing in some line or paying a fortune to some divorce attorney for a divorce. It becomes a follow the crowd thing. Recently, I heard of a woman who was diagnosed with cancer that was missed early on because of some squabble with an insurance company over what testing was necessary. One thing I learned from that scary situation is that I can reserve the right to pay for testing myself if I feel it's needed. As a successful survivor of early cancer detection, I've learned that the last thing I want to do is put my health and peace of mind in the hands of someone trying to cut costs for an insurance company.

Those who stand to lead this world through change and progress day-to-day will be those people willing to push the envelope, make decisions, create better solutions, question status quo, and make discoveries in an honest and sincere way. Asking *why* and *how else* and not settling for less, even if others do, are keys for getting the most out of life. We need to take responsibility to critically evaluate current thinking, think for ourselves, trust our gut, and give ourselves permission to expect better.

The tricky part is figuring out *when* to follow conventional approaches and *when* to dare to try to find a better alternative. Be sure of this one very important thing: people like you and me make discoveries every single day on better ways to exist in our world. We can wait for others to fill us in or we can jump right in and help find out faster. Taking charge is for everyone. Achieving a better life is about a deep personal commitment to ourselves and the world in which we live. The good news is we get to practice taking charge to create our own luck every single day. With that kind of practice, we should get pretty good at it, then pass it on!

LESSON #91

THE BALANCING ACT

As a kid, I can remember watching the old *Ed Sullivan Show*. It was a variety show that featured lots of different, new, and interesting talent. I remember being fascinated by a person spinning four plates on top of separate sticks. I loved watching him figure out *precisely* how long he had to get four plates spinning while making it back in the knick of time to catch that first plate before it fell.

I've become a fan of *precision* in life as a way to have it all. Having it all may seem unachievable, but with balance and skill we can successfully achieve what's important to us before it's too late.

One example I love, to replace the four spinning plates, is our approach to balancing family, coupleness, work, future, and individuality. Often I'll ask audiences how they would prioritize these five important life priorities. Naturally, there are many different combinations as potential answers. It's not so much about what your combination is today, it's really about the *order* you give to your priorities. Perhaps in your mind, you may say family is first. Let's say then that maybe individuality falls last. What I share with people is the danger of a top and bottom to our list. Typically, the most neglected part of any list will be the bottom. The problem is that you run the risk of getting burned out by neglecting your own needs.

What about if we replace that top to bottom list with a picture of five spinning plates? Now we've eliminated a *top and bottom list*. What we now have are five equally important priorities all spinning on the same level horizontally. It's this different perspective and picture in our own minds that allows us to look at our *plates* equally. It allows us to be like that plate spinner who's learned to develop precision and timing to make sure all five plates stay in the air. I love it! What a great argument for quality time and having it all.

When raising a family or working hard, it's so easy to neglect our coupleness or individuality. I've always held that before ever becoming someone's spouse or parent was an individual who was alive and well. We need to be careful not to lose sight of that individual with wants and needs for personal achievement. At the same time, it's so easy to stop being a couple because we're being pulled in ten different directions at once. When we stop spinning that *couple plate*, there's trouble a brewin' if it falls to the bottom of the list.

It seems that in this Superman and Superwoman world we may be trying too hard to be all things to all people. Maybe we're on permanent overload and have no time to reflect on what happens next. Our strategy is keeping up rather than planning ahead for our future. We're not taking the time to figure out what's important and what's not. It's very sad indeed when families rarely sit together for an unrushed family dinner that includes good, old-fashioned *Ozzie & Harriet* conversation. Impossible, you say? Not so fast. A town in New Jersey actually voted to have one Tuesday evening as an unscheduled evening throughout the town. I love it! What cracks me up is that the town had to propose it. Are we nuts? Or, are we lost?

Let's get back on track. Let's get some balance, for goodness sake. Life has a way of getting away from all of us sometimes. It's up to us to stop the *rat race* and *put the brakes on* to give ourselves and our families the quality time they deserve. Confident decision making will bring back some real balance to our lives. We can do that by starting to say no to some things. Let's get those schedules adjusted. Let's stop the kid and taxi rat race. What are we doing to ourselves and our kids when we have no time to chill out, no down time, no time to reflect, and no time to plan ahead? Are we really teaching our kids the best habits when we're racing all over creation trying to be all things to all people? Unwinding and personal quiet time *daily* are keys to reducing stress and bringing balance to a hectic lifestyle. Just because we can, doesn't mean we should do all the things we try to do. Yes, we can be stretching beyond our limits and appearing to hold up pretty well, but no longer enjoying life like we should. The good news is that once we become aware of it, we've taken step one to pulling in the reins.

LESSON #92

BUILDING BETTER HABITS

Taking the time to build winning habits can sometimes feel discouraging. With the best plan, it can be disappointing and make us feel inadequate. Woulda, coulda, and shoulda are words that represent the best of intentions. We've all heard people with good intentions say things like, "I've got to start exercising." "I have just got to lose weight." "I have just got to get organized." and "I've just got to stop wasting time." All too often though, not much changes. However, there are some great tips that can help us achieve better results. I'll share some of what I've discovered about successfully creating new habits.

Several years ago, we had an aging dog that began waking us up many times during the night to go out. One time, when bringing the dog to the vet, I asked if there was anything he recommended to reduce her nightly trips. He asked when we fed her. After telling him we always fed her at about dinnertime (for 12 years), he suggested we begin feeding her in the morning instead. Why didn't I think of *that* myself? On my way home from the vet, I began getting excited about the possibility of success and getting some sleep at night. Now, what I discovered was that this new idea was easy to remember for the first few days. Then after awhile, after dinner, my husband and I would look at each other and ask, "Did you feed the dog?" And, we would feel so bad when we forgot. Yes, a relapse was in full swing, and oh, our poor dog! To make sure I remembered, I decided to come up with a foolproof gimmick to remind me to feed the dog during my morning routine. I came up with a simple 4" x 6" card on my bathroom counter that I left in plain view so I wouldn't ever forget. It worked like a charm. I've heard that it takes 21 days to create a new habit, but what I discovered is it can take a lot longer than that before something becomes a comfortable part of a changed routine. I bet it took a couple of months using my bathroom card gimmick before I successfully trained myself to consistently remember to feed the dog in the morning.

Another time, about 10 years ago, I impulsively decided to buy a new treadmill. How many of you dust yours off along with cleaning your house? After the purchase and delivery, my brother happened to stop in and I excitedly bragged about my new purchase. His next comment to me was, "You'll be done with it in three weeks so I'll take it off your hands after that." My first impulse was to be insulted, but deep down I wondered if he might be right. He really provided me with what I call *healthy fear*. Sure enough, my intentions were golden. I'd get up in the morning and tell myself I'd do this, that, and the other, then I'd do the treadmill. Somehow I would make a deal with myself to do the really important stuff first, but then I'd skip the exercise.

I discovered that once I got on a roll for the day, my great intentions began to fade before my eyes. So, I came up with another gimmick. I told myself that I would *not even look* at my to-do list until after I exercised. What I discovered was that, when adding in a habit that has never been done before, top placement is critical for success. In order to develop the exercise habit, I had to bite the bullet and force myself to exercise first thing in the morning. While this may seem simple, it was in fact harder to do than I would have thought. But, I stuck it out. Over the course of three to six months of implementing this new daily ritual, it began to feel routine. The consuming thoughts of worry over delaying calls, tasks, and projects subsided.

While I honestly doubted my own ability, I was quite happy about being able to pull it off. When it comes to exercise, it's so easy to use other priorities to squeeze this one out. I had come to a point, with my children grown and gone, that I knew deep down I had run out of excuses, but I wasn't at all sure I could pull it off. After all, exercise is not something we yearn for until it becomes a comfortable habit.

This lesson is about learning that changing habits or anything else is never easy. It takes some planning and obstacle removal when relapse occurs. *I realized that I needed to give top priority to the new habit until it became familiar and comfortable.* I also learned that reminders or gimmicks are essential to create early success and prevent disappointing ourselves or relapsing again.

This lesson points out the importance of becoming *change-hardy,* by regularly challenging ourselves to do something differently. It's great practice for building adaptability. So what's your most recent change or new habit? Are there some you haven't yet moved from fantasyland to reality? You're in charge. Think about what your pitfalls are, prioritize, and use gimmicks to help you. Then, you're on your way to building winning habits.

LESSON #93

AN IDEA IS ONLY AS GOOD AS
THE PERSON WHO GETS BEHIND IT

There are two pictures that come to my mind when I wonder about great ideas. One is the *pet rock* from some years ago and the other is *bottled water*. In today's world, we sure can learn a lot from bottled water. First of all, I'd like to know who dreamed up the idea of selling bottled water. Can you imagine taking your best friend into confidence and secretly telling that you've come up with a great idea to bottle water and then sell it for a dollar or two? Even the loyalty of best friends wouldn't prevent them from wondering if you've lost it with a ridiculous idea like *people paying for water*.

Selling bottled water is an incredible example to show that any idea is only as good as the commitment of the person who gets behind it. "Fly me to the moon and let me sit among the stars"...on bottled water? Who would ever have guessed that one? Now it's become cool to walk around with a bottle of water. It must be "cool," because it's caught on.

Let this be a simple lesson to us all. Fame and fortune for each of us can be as simple as selling bottled water, if you're the first to make it happen. The interesting part of this example is that while most of us would have laughed at the idea, some people didn't. And those *same people* were all it took to get the idea off the ground. After you get your idea to the right customers and sales are pouring in, the laughing stops!

We get ideas from people all the time. We often discount them without giving them a try, or we discount them after obstacle number one appears. It makes me wonder whether the idea wasn't good, or was it the lack of commitment by the person implementing it? The goal with any raw idea is to make it your own and ultimately make it better than it was when you got it. Hand-me-downs will always be hand-me-downs. Custom tailoring will always make a difference in the fit of any idea. *What you put into the idea is as valuable an ingredient as the idea itself.* Let's not forget our personal responsibility to work at something long enough to make it work for us. Discounting the knowledge, wisdom, and experience of others can prevent us from advancing in the Game of Life.

LESSON #94

BE CAREFUL WHO YOU LISTEN TO

Picture a person who is thinking about doing something, when all of a sudden a devil appears on their left shoulder and begins whispering into their ear with negative feedback. For example, blame someone, get even, don't waste your time, or don't bother. Then, all of a sudden, an angel appears on their right shoulder and starts giving advice that comes from caring and honoring others. And, let's say that the angel stopped appearing because the person never took that advice. What a sad state of affairs would face them, because the devil on their left shoulder now controls them in destructive ways.

One thing that'll never change, regardless of how many books a person reads or classes and seminars a person attends, is the fact that we're all human beings. The human preference is the path of least resistance. It takes a lot of angels to even budge us to the better good. When all we know is destructive people, it becomes more difficult to pave the way for better alternatives. When what we know mostly comes from people who are constructive, then we build the odds for our own success.

Follow-the-leader was a game we all played as kids. We tried to keep up and do what those ahead of us did. Even though we followed, there was a certain challenge in being able to keep up. This lesson is really about the relationships we foster in our day-to-day undertakings. Do we hang out with the best possible winning people, or do we find our way to the bottom of the pile so we can feel less threatened?

None of us is perfect, but how we establish our own personal performance standards can be reflected in the people with whom we surround ourselves. In my early career, I was extremely fortunate to have rubbed elbows with some winners who became my leaders to follow. What they did looked doable to me, and so I followed. In my early sales career I had the privilege to follow Lauraine Blier, who brought integrity, class, and dignity to great sales success. Following in her footsteps became my performance standard until I was able to create my own. Lucky me! It was almost a no-brainer. Next, I had the privilege of working with Tommy Damigella. His winning approach and guidance kept me from abandoning my goals and jumping ship many times in my climb through sales success in the '70s. There was no one else in my life at that time providing that kind of day-to-day effort to guide me and my career. With his unselfish help and support, a butterfly emerged from a cocoon and flew away with a new set of personal and professional performance standards. Lucky me! There are *so many* winners I've had the great fortune to meet. Each has been like an exciting book that I get to learn and take from in my pursuit for the best, as I upgrade my own personal performance standards.

I love winners. They're the people who successfully get out of their own way, make things happen, wake up and grab life, don't make excuses, want it all, dance through their lives, and give meaning to the lives of others! They are the people who make a difference in our world. They care about others and pass on their knowledge and wisdom. Life is a choice. You handpick the leaders you follow. Their standards become your standards, their voice becomes your thoughts, and your thoughts create your behavior, WIN OR LOSE! You become like those you hang around with. Winners are "angels" we need to hang out with and listen to.

LESSON #95

EASY STREET

Easy Street is not complacency. Complacency is when we get too comfortable and neglect the winner within. Complacency is an unwillingness to try something new or push ourselves. Complacency prevents us from making the sacrifices necessary to advance to a better position and extricate ourselves from a bad one. Complacency leads to dependence. An example of excessive dependence is a battered woman who freely chooses to stay with the man who beats her on a regular basis. While the rest of us who aren't excessively dependent can't understand why such individuals don't leave, the truth is their dependent position has taken away their ability to make decisions and use logic.

Ever wonder how much time we spend trying to make sure we don't extend ourselves unnecessarily? Take a look at the workplace. It's filled with people doing as little as possible and wanting as much as possible in return. They keep a sharp eye out to avoid *anything* extra. While complacency may feel easy, it really is a path to unhappiness and burnout in the big picture.

Personal achievement and personal pride, not complacency, are the directions to Easy Street. They are the reasons we exist. They give us value. They are the cornerstone of healthy self-esteem. They make us feel important in our world. They develop our ability to continue unlocking our treasure chest of talent. While we all need to relax and cut ourselves some slack at times, it is *our* responsibility to give our lives meaning and value in whatever task, work, or role we assume. Sometimes I wonder if we've gotten our *guard up* against anything that feels too hard. All we have to do is believe in possibility and our own ability to rise to the occasion. I wonder if age creeps in as a factor to becoming complacent. That is, "I'm too old for that now." Complacency can drain a person's enthusiasm for life. It can rob our focus.

This lesson is about guarding against letting complacency take over our attitudes and put us on a fast track to burnout and stress. Remember the advice from Lesson #40 about picturing yourself a winner, "I don't care if you shovel garbage, shovel it better than anyone ever shoveled it." One thing is for sure, winners are not complacent. Focusing on our ability to make things happen is a deterrent to complacency. Leaving our comfort zones and making discoveries are great deterrents to complacency. Helping others and not focusing solely on ourselves are great deterrents to complacency.

There are people everywhere in the workplace who are absolutely miserable and believe they have no choices. They could very well be victims of complacency. I remember stories over the years about Wall Street financial wizards who give it all up to go live in the wilderness, for goodness sakes. Complacency can lock us in indecision and a victim mentality. The longer we subject ourselves to it, the more we can adversely affect our own wellness. Complacency can hold us hostage. We become dependent on misery. We become unable to make decisions to change the misery.

There is always a way out. There is always a choice. Just because something is tough is not a reason to run the other way. As a matter of fact, it just might be the stretch you need to begin moving forward and living again on Easy Street.

LESSON #96

PERFECTIONISTS ARE NOT...

You've got to know the difference between when perfect is necessary and good enough is okay. This lesson is a study of personal rigidity and the inability to let something slide. Know any perfectionists? The fascinating thing to me about perfectionists is that they are extremely talented, bright, and insightful people when it comes to setting standards. However, there's one thing perfectionists are *not*. They're not good at *coping*.

Rather than becoming the standard bearers, perfectionists become people we choose to avoid because nothing is ever good enough. They basically see the world as inadequate overall. They spend their lives confronting and correcting the wrongs of others in pursuit of perfection. The perfectionist will die *never* achieving that goal. Perfectionists have a way of turning people off, but don't realize it. Their rigidity causes people to steer away from them like the plague.

One sales manager I can recall during my career was a perfectionist. It seemed that her goal in life was to find something wrong with everyone and everything, and then point it out. Absolutely *nothing* was allowed to slide. It became a real problem to receive her daily phone calls. One staff member would say to another, "I talked to her yesterday. You talk to her today." It had come to the point that virtually no one in my office wanted anything to do with her. She came to represent *the ugly*. The interesting part was that my office staff bent over backwards to help people. They were wonderful. However, every phone call from this perfectionist *deflated* them, one at a time. She would take the time to point out the insignificant. She would make a mountain out of a molehill. She kept a scorecard on everyone. She had *no clue* that our scorecard for her had become zero. Yes, you guessed it. Confrontation finally was her downfall and she became the weakest link. She had become poison in the organization. My guess is that she found new venues in which to carry out her war against the inadequate world she lived in. But, thankfully for us, our war with the perfectionist was over. We survive perfectionists, but we don't learn much from them except to not be like them.

The very sad part about this lesson is that this perfectionist was a very talented person. Sadly, she had a terribly negative impact on the world she wanted to perfect. This person was constantly battling someone. It was as if she had a rotating list of people to take issue with. I'm not sure if she ever realized how toxic she became to those around her.

This lesson has served as a reminder to me over the years to be vigilant and aware of when perfect is necessary or good enough is okay. Balancing high standards with learning when to let go of the insignificant is not always easy. We've got to learn to channel our energy into the productive rather than the unproductive, while developing the wisdom to know the difference.

I can remember times in my career as an executive when it seemed like negatives were all we were dealing with. When I'd find myself getting to that point, I remember deliberately stopping myself from getting sucked in. I'd say, "Unless the roof falls in, I'm letting this slide." I instinctively knew when there needed to be a "climate change." I suppose it's the ratio of positives to negatives. The positives have to far outweigh the negatives in order to create some level of cooperation with others. It is so easy for whatever reason to let the negatives take the lead. There will always be plenty to complain about if that becomes our focus. Taking the critical or negative role is a path that leads us further and further from the good. Ultimately, we will hurt ourselves with personal stress and burnout.

This same example can apply to our family climates. Have we gotten ourselves to the point that our children fear us? Are we constantly pointing out weaknesses? Maybe we've become perfectionists in our view of how others ought to be. Maybe it's time for a *climate adjustment* if conversation has become more negative than positive. Perfection in brain surgery and rocket science are necessary. But there are many other things in life that are clearly not so urgent or critical as to require the perfection that some of us might impose. In order to lead, we've got to develop our *ability to relate* to those whom we wish to have follow our lead.

LESSON #97

DARE TO BE DIFFERENT

Success comes from assessing your environment and instinctively discovering what might be missing that you can capitalize on to distinguish yourself from the pack. And, you're probably going to go it alone. I've often said that were I to go into any different field or profession, the first thing I would find out is where the weakness is and begin by eliminating that weakness with my approach.

Let's say, for example, that I went into the real estate business. It has always amazed me that once a home is sold, there's not so much as a thank you note or house-warming gift sent by the profiting agent. While customers aren't exactly waiting for a present, I've often regarded this oversight as an opportunity lost by real estate people. While buying or selling a home is not always a fun thing, you'd always want *the last thing* remembered by the customer to be a positive one. It's the "kiss and make up" part of business dealings. It's ensuring the last thing a customer remembers is very positive and thoughtful. It's what sets the next stage.

I remember buying our home some years ago. We waltzed into an open house with no agent representing us to claim half the commission when we made our offer. It was easy and simple for the seller's agent. Once the contract was signed, we were history. They were out of the loop. I remember thinking how disconnected that agent was from our excitement over buying this new house. That memory has always stuck with me. If I were ever to sell real estate, the first thing I would promise myself is to have my customers remember me in a positive and surprising way after the business part concluded. Imagine if a real estate agent took the time to find out when moving day was and brought or sent food over on that day? Imagine if a lovely houseplant arrived for you on moving day? Impact is so powerful when we do something nice that is unexpected. People in the workplace so easily brush off an opportunity to distinguish themselves. Yet, it's the small piece that ties it all together to separate them from the rest. It leaves that perception that becomes the *stimulus* for future business.

When we *dare to be different*, it should never be about grandstanding or elevating ourselves above others but, rather, elevating our standards above the current standards of operation. Daring to be different is our expectation to learn from the world around us and aspire to make that world better by adding our *special touch*. It's about expecting more of ourselves than others may expect of us. It's our ability to distinguish ourselves, to set new standards from which others may learn. It's our commitment to make our little piece of life the absolute best it can be. It's climbing to the peak when the world is laughing. It is our own journey to be the best we can be and then to pass it on.

LESSON #98

IF I ALWAYS DO
WHAT I'VE ALWAYS DONE

If I always do what I've always done, then I'll always get what I've always gotten. It's your quick and easy recipe for repeating history. Don't change a thing. If you're *happy* with history, then keep doing what you're doing. If you're *not happy* with it, then don't keep doing what you're doing when it's not working.

You don't have to look too much further than a New Year's resolution to see how real this can be. Let me pose this interesting question to you. When do people typically begin dieting? If Monday is your answer, you're probably thinking what many think. Now my next question is, when do diets typically relapse? I know. It's the first day the office decides to order out from a new restaurant, or someone finally brings in that recipe they've bragged about for six months. Don't you just hate it? How could Murphy's Law be so cruel? And, just when you were *really* serious this time.

Well, there are many scenarios in life that illustrate our struggle with the trap called "that always happens." So, in this lesson, we need to put our thinking caps on. Rethink the pitfalls and real life solutions that allow us to be better prepared. One thing for sure is obstacles will be there. In our quest to pick the perfect Monday to start dieting with a motivated mindset, we sometimes forget to include the problem solving that corrects past mistakes, pitfalls, or relapses. Here's where courage, determination, and persistence come into play. We've got to have the courage to change what doesn't work rather than hope it doesn't happen. We've got to have the determination to get better solutions than the ones that haven't worked. We've got to be persistent in removing obstacles, one success at a time. And, please don't feel guilty because some things you try don't work. Feeling too guilty derails our focus and goals and can end up in the "why bother?" trash can.

Every year people face budgets that may fall short. Yet, year in and year out, not much changes. Perhaps the slippery slope gets slightly more slippery. This lesson is certainly not about being embarrassed or feeling stupid about a predicament you face. It's about coming to grips with the fact that *every day offers opportunity* to come up with a successful plan to change your course. It's about examining what you're happy with and what you'd like to improve. The real problem is when we allow one day, one month, or one year to just roll into the next, without facing up to the reality that is catching up with us quickly. It's not about being perfect. It's about catching something before negative consequences occur.

It's always been amazing to me how many possibilities and opportunities we have to make improvements. Advice and knowledge are everywhere. Great examples are everywhere. The only ingredient we need to add is our personal commitment to want to take a better path on our journey through this Game of Life.

If I always do what I've always done, then I'll always get what I've always gotten. It's a decision to *let it ride* or *wake up* and begin making the winning changes for a winning outcome to change history. Check your treasure chest and fish under a couple of things. I'm sure you're packing what you need to get it done. Stop feeling guilty if something you try doesn't turn to gold.

LESSON #99

WINNING IS NOT WHAT
THE WORLD GIVES YOU
IT'S WHAT YOU GIVE YOURSELF

What ignites that spark in you? For me, it was the determination to change the course of history for my family by extricating ourselves from the ravages of poverty. It was my pursuit to give life meaning. It was my *what if* curiosity about exploring possibilities and self-discovery. It was longing to have what I saw others enjoy. It was my frustration at watching my own parents suffering through alcoholism and near destruction. It was the embarrassment of feeling the limitations that seemed *invisibly* imposed in my formative years. It was getting out of my own way without resenting my past. It was the freedom I felt as an adult to take charge of my own destiny. It was about shortening the distance from Point A to Point B.

Tom Damigella has said that his family relocated from Italy to America because his mother had typhoid fever. Having to leave their roots in Italy to begin again in America allowed him to get a college education. That separated him from the pack in the '30s when only a small percentage of people had college educations. The birth of plastic in the late '40s gave him the chance to become a groundbreaker and pioneer with Earl Tupper to create Tupperware Home Parties in the '50s. He found his open door to opportunity when I was just three years old. Little did I know that he was birthing my opportunity for some 22 years later, when I followed through that same door of opportunity.

At age 25, for the first time in my life, I discovered I had a treasure chest. I found the winners I needed to help me break out of my cocoon. Without their winning influence, success might have eluded me. Once I learned winner thinking and successfully replaced the old loser thinking with the new winner thinking, I was able to move forward. I learned to value my roots and use my own wings. I learned how to get out of my own way, make it happen, take charge, focus, and open doors.

During my very successful 30 years as an entrepreneur, I remember getting the feeling that I wasn't done yet. I've gotten used to that feeling. It's really that natural homegrown curiosity about what we're capable of and passionate about doing next. It's that openness to achieve greater things. It prevents us from getting stuck. I don't worry so much anymore because I've armed myself with winner thinking. I've surrounded myself with winners, and I've long ago realized that I can't wait to be spoon-fed. The world doesn't revolve around me. I take charge to create my own opportunity and open my own doors. Now, I share it with you.

I've developed a real passion for bringing out the best in others and uncovering the winner within. I know too well how easy it would have been for me to miss it all. Winning and success can come from the most unlikely places and the most unlikely people in the most unlikely situations. We *do* have a responsibility to pass it on and help others figure it out by giving back some of what we've been so fortunate to discover and achieve. My goal is always to help people *think for themselves,* so they can overcome their own challenges and move themselves forward. If I've helped pull open a door for you or turn on a light of knowledge, then great!

You don't owe me a thing. I've been there, too. If you want to pay me back, then don't let the chain of success end with you.

LESSON #100

LIVING YOUR DREAMS

You're a take charge person and deserve the best
Even when your life is put to the test.

Learning to win and continuing to grow
Is not an accident but a choice you know.

So set your goals high, hook your wagon to a star,
The stretch and the ride will build who you are.

As the goals you set get higher and higher,
That adrenaline pumping will set you on fire.

You see, my treasure was buried down deep too
And maybe I can help search for yours with you.

Life becomes a struggle that's hard to beat
Living day to day just to make ends meet.

You see, the future is bright, as bright as the sun
Let the past be, the best is yet to come!

Winning can be learned, it's not so unique
I hope I've given you a little peek

At how to take charge and what it means
To *win at life* by living your dreams!

LESSON #101

THE ENVELOPE PLEASE

AND THE
WINNER IS:

Okay, here's where you get to fill in the blanks. You've seen the common thread throughout these lessons. I've put my heart and soul into clarifying some of the issues that were far from clear to me as I made my way along. I've honored those who've created my defining moments of development. Now it's time to ignite your own spark to win and become the winner you deserve to be. You're on a winning team. The clock is ticking. The starting gun is about to be fired. On your mark, get set, go!

"If life's a relay, then here's your baton.
Run with it, my friend, and pass it on!"

WINNING <u>IS</u> CONTAGIOUS!

Book Order Form

Honor Someone You Care About
Unique Gifts For Special People And Special Occasions

SHIP TO: (Please Include Phone # Or E-Mail Address)

_____

_____

_____

_____

Call or Fax this form to: 716-688-5507
E-Mail order: winningtrackpress@att.net
Mail to: Winning Track Press
P. O. Box 204
East Amherst, New York 14051

_____ # of Books at $19.95 each $_____
(Call For Volume Discounts)
Shipping: $4.00 for the first book and
$1.00 for each additional $_____

Subtotal $_____
Make Check Payable To: Tax 8%
Winning Track Press   (NY Only) $_____

Credit Card #:   **Total** $_____

— — — — — — — — — — — — — — — —

Exp: ___ ___   *Name on Card:*_____